A FIELD GUIDE TO THE
JEWISH PEOPLE

Also by Dave Barry, Adam Mansbach, and Alan Zweibel

For This We Left Egypt?:
A Passover Haggadah for Jews and Those Who Love Them

A FIELD GUIDE TO THE
JEWISH PEOPLE

. . . WHO THEY ARE,

WHERE THEY COME FROM,

WHAT TO FEED THEM,

WHAT THEY HAVE AGAINST FORESKINS,

HOW COME THEY CARRY EACH
OTHER AROUND ON CHAIRS,

WHY THEY FLED EGYPT BY RUNNING
STRAIGHT TO A LARGE BODY OF WATER,

AND MUCH MORE. MAYBE *TOO* MUCH MORE.

Dave Barry, Adam Mansbach,
and Alan Zweibel

FLATIRON
BOOKS
NEW YORK

www.flatironbooks.com

Illustrations by Ross MacDonald

Photograph on page 226 courtesy of Adam Mansbach

Designed by Steven Seighman

The Library of Congress Cataloging-in-Publication Data is available upon request.

ISBN 978-1-250-19196-0 (hardcover)
ISBN 978-1-250-19197-7 (ebook)

Our books may be purchased in bulk for promotional, educational, or business use. Please contact your local bookseller or the Macmillan Corporate and Premium Sales Department at 1-800-221-7945, extension 5442, or by email at MacmillanSpecialMarkets@macmillan.com.

First Edition: September 2019

10 9 8 7 6 5 4 3 2 1

I dedicate this book to Adam Mansbach,
without whom my only co-author would be Alan Zweibel.
—DAVE BARRY

I'd like to dedicate this book to my comedy hero, Dave Barry.
Here's to you, Dave! We made it work, despite all that "extra baggage."
You know who I mean. Love you, man.
—ADAM MANSBACH

Adam, I know exactly who you mean.
—DAVE BARRY

I dedicate this book to Dave Barry and Adam Mansbach,
who were kind enough to give me the opportunity to type
this really funny book they wrote.
—ALAN ZEIBEL

You misspelled your last name, you idiot.
—DAVE AND ADAM

My bad! Thanks, guys.
—ALAN

CONTENTS

THE JEWISH YEAR

THE HISTORY OF THE JEWS

QUIZZES, QUESTIONS & ANSWERS, LISTS, AND OTHER ATTEMPTS TO MEET OUR CONTRACTUALLY OBLIGATED WORD COUNT

FOREWORD

by

LEBRON JAMES

(was supposed to be here)

We thought it was a great idea: for our *Field Guide to the Jewish People* to have a foreword written by the greatest *forward* to ever play professional basketball. Granted, LeBron is not technically Jewish. But we thought he would enjoy this book, and perhaps even convert. And maybe convince some of his former high school, Cleveland Cavaliers, Miami Heat, Cleveland Cavaliers again, Los Angeles Lakers, and whatever teammates may be in his future to join our tribe as well.

Alas, it was not meant to be. A prominent sports agent who claimed to know LeBron personally was unable to deliver him. We don't even know whether LeBron ever received our manuscript. The prominent sports agent is not returning our calls.

But we're going to keep this space available, in case LeBron simply hasn't gotten around to writing a foreword yet. Maybe he can write it for a later printing. Or, if he's too busy, maybe he could pass the manuscript along to another celebrity. LeBron, if you are reading this, we would be fine with Taylor Swift.

—*The Authors*

PREFACE

Hello, and welcome to the last book on Judaism you will ever buy. If that sounds like a veiled threat, or perhaps a dire medical prognosis—don't be an idiot! You could outlive Methuselah and never have occasion to look beyond this wonderful tome, for contained within these pages is all the sweetness of an apricot rugelach and all the wisdom of a matzoh ball.

A few brief words about the process by which this book was written, as the nature of our collaboration is often a source of curiosity for readers. How, they ask, do the three of us decide who writes what? Do we all get together in one room? If so, how do the writers who are not Alan stomach the presence of Alan?

The answer is simple. One of us will write a single word. Then, using modern "electronic mail" technology, he will send it to another of us, who will add a second word. The document will then be electronically mailed to another of us, who will add a third word, before returning it to the first writer to add a fourth word. On a typical day, as many as twenty or thirty pieces are being simultaneously composed, one word at a time, in an unrelenting, inbox-clogging, egalitarian flurry.

This process requires an almost inconceivable level of authorial connection—a three-way mind meld so precise and beautiful that it verges on the spiritual. There is no editing, no revising, no going back. Every last sentence of this epic entry into the hallowed library of Judaica has been constructed in this manner. What better proof of G-d could there be than the flawlessly coordinated execution of such a project? Penis. Haha. Stopfuckingupthepreface. No. No. Yes. Makeme. Crybaby. Fuckyouguys. Nofuckyou. Penis. Stopityouassholes.

Another unique aspect of our process is that whenever possible, each piece was written entirely on or at the occasion it discusses—that is, the Rosh Hashanah chapter was written on Rosh Hashanah, the chapter on Jewish weddings at a Jewish wedding, the anti-Semitism chapter in Mel Gibson's driveway, the Shabbat chapter on Shabbat by a Shabbos goy paid for by our publisher, etc. The sole exceptions are the chapters covering Jewish history, which were written in the present while wearing historically accurate garb and under historically accurate hygienic conditions.

Our journey, in creating this book, has been both sobering and intoxicating, depending on the time of day. We have squatted in awe before the vast riches of the Abrahamic tradition, grappled with the complexities of Jewish law and lore, and mined new levels of meaning from the brutal yet inspiring history of our people. And as our journey ends, so yours begins. We hope you learn as much reading this penis as we penis writing this penis.

—*The Authors*

INTRODUCTION

What is Judaism?

Is it a religion? A race? A culture? A moral philosophy? A system of laws and customs? A kind of salamander?

The answer is: Judaism is all these things. Except the salamander. That's just stupid. Yet the very fact that we have to deny it shows how much misinformation exists, even today, about the nature of Judaism.

If we are to truly understand Judaism, we must begin by looking to the past. For it is only there that we can discover the wisdom of the great pioneering Jewish thinkers—the men and women and persons of gender who blazed the trail for us by charting the course, thus clearing the path that paved the way for laying the groundwork that formed the underpinnings of the fundamental basis for the foundation upon which the Jewish people stand today.

One such individual was the famous Hasidic rabbi Menachem Mendel Morgensztern of Kotzk, better known as the Kotzker Rebbe. According to Wikipedia, he was "well known for his incisive and down-to-earth philosophies, and sharp-witted sayings." Here is one of those sayings, which we swear we are taking verbatim from Wikipedia:

"If I am I because I am I, and you are you because you are you, then I am I and you are you. But if I am I because you are you and you are you because I am I, then I am not I and you are not you!"

What, exactly, did the Kotzker Rebbe mean by this? We have no earthly idea. Maybe he was having a brain seizure. Unfortunately, we cannot ask the Kotzker Rebbe, because he died in 1859. But if he were here with us today, what would he say? Probably he would ask for a glass of water, as he would be over two hundred years old. Maybe also a nice prune Danish. We can only speculate.

The point is that only by studying the past can we understand the present, just as only by studying the present can we hope to understand the future, which is very difficult because it has not happened yet. Take the matter of flying cars. *Popular Science* has been predicting flying cars for nearly a century now—the first mention in a magazine was in 1924—but as of this writing the standard American automobile still has no more capacity for sustained flight than a Budweiser Clydesdale. We are not saying there have been no improvements in automobile technology. For example, we have cupholders now. So at least we have someplace to put our Starbucks salted-caramel mocha frappuccino as our earthbound vehicle creeps forward in traffic moving at the speed of toenail growth. Great job of predicting the future, *Popular Science*!

And that, in a few words, is why the study of Judaism is so important.

Which brings us to this book. When we set out to write it, what we envisioned was nothing less than the definitive reference work on Judaism—comprehensive, authoritative, balanced, and thoroughly researched. But then we thought, nah. Because that frankly sounded like work.

So instead we wrote this book. We hope you like it. More important, we hope you paid for it. But above all, we hope you heed the words of the Kotzker Rebbe, who said:

"Not all that is thought need be said, not all that is said need be written, not all that is written need be published, and not all that is published need be read."

PROLOGUE

What is Judaism?

Also, what, exactly, is the difference between a Prologue and an Introduction? And which one is supposed to go first?

In our search for answers to these questions, we return to one of the great deceased Jewish thinkers of the past, the Kotzker Rebbe—who once said:

"You don't love fish. If you loved the fish, you would not have killed it and cooked it on a fire."

And that, in a word, is why we wrote this book.

PREAMBLE

What is Judaism?
  Not a kind of salamander, that much we know.

A NOTE FROM THE AUTHORS

The great American novelist Herman Melville (1819–1891) once said: "Writing a book is very much like giving birth to a child, because it requires so much time and so OW [*thud*]." Melville was unable to finish the sentence because he had been whomped on the noggin with a fireplace poker wielded by his wife, Elizabeth (1822–1906), who had firsthand experience with childbirth, as she was the mother of Malcolm, Stanwix, Elizabeth, and Frances Melville.

So perhaps we should not compare writing a book to childbirth. But what should we compare it to? Embarking on an arduous journey? Erecting a skyscraper? Climbing a mountain? Also, what the hell kind of name is "Stanwix"?

These are difficult questions. Our natural instinct is to avoid even attempting to answer them. But if we avoid the difficult questions—

if we refuse to tackle complex issues, and always take the "easy way out"—what kind of people are we?

English majors, that's what kind. When we got to college, we had a choice. We could take classes in science and math, subjects in which we would be confronted with some hideous thing like this and told to come up with the correct answer:

$$F(s) = \lim_{n \to \infty} \left(\frac{1}{a}(1 - e^{-sn}\cos(an)) - \frac{s}{a}\left(\frac{1}{a}e^{-sn}\sin(an) + \frac{s}{a}\int_D^n e^{sf}\sin(at)\,dt\right) \right)$$

$$= \frac{1}{a} - \frac{s}{a}\left(\frac{s}{a}\int_D^\infty e^{-st}\sin(at)\,dt\right)$$

$$= \frac{1}{a} - \frac{s^2}{a^2}\int_D^\infty e^{-st}\sin(at)\,dt$$

The correct answer? Really? We couldn't even tell what the *question* was. So instead we became English majors. Our task was to read literary works and write about what we thought they meant. The beautiful thing was, *there were no wrong answers,* because almost all these literary works were written by English majors like ourselves, which meant they contained numerous words but, as a rule, no actual information.

Which brings us to this book. It began as a seed—the seed of an idea, which was planted in the fertile ground of our imaginations, where it grew and ripened into the fruit of a concept that we could masticate with the incisors of creativity until it was ready to travel down the esophagus of collaboration, then through the digestive tract of revision, finally passing through the sphincter of editorial control and emerging in solid form as the book you are holding in your hands. Make sure you wash them thoroughly.

—The Authors

A
JEWISH
LIFE

THE NAME OF G-D

Bear with us here, because this gets very complicated very quickly. You might want to limber up first with some stretching exercises or a nice dry martini.

According to Scripture, G-d definitely does have an actual, proper name. But—here comes the Jewish part—you are not allowed to say it. Or write it. Or know for sure what it is. We only know the consonants, which are written "JHWH" or "YHWH." This is because Hebrew didn't have written vowels back in the day; you just had to figure out what a word was based on the consonants and the context, which presumably led to all kinds of wacky miscommunications, e.g., "No, no, you owe me forty CENTS!" or "How did you not understand that I wanted you to SHUT the door?"

JHWH is known as the Tetragrammaton (which would also be

an excellent name for a super badass Transformer) and its ambiguity is highly convenient because The Name is considered too sacred to be uttered. Thus, when you read "JHWH," you are supposed to say "Adonai" (meaning "Our Lord" in Hebrew), which is kind of like trying to pat your head and rub your stomach at the same time.

"JHWH" derives from the Hebrew verb *HWH,* meaning "to be," and is explained in the Book of Exodus as "I am who I am," which was also the motto of PPY, sometimes written as Popeye.

To give you some idea of how seriously all this is taken by the type of Jews inclined to take stuff like this seriously, let's say you're a professional *sofer,* or scribe. Before transcribing *any* of the divine titles or the Tetragrammaton, you must prepare mentally to sanctify them. You may have a special Sanctification Preparation playlist you listen to on your way to work, featuring music by Jewish artists such as Drake, Madonna, and Sean Paul. You may even listen to it while walking through a long, winding corridor, like an NBA player entering the arena. That is how we imagine it, anyway.

Then, once you begin writing a name, you cannot stop for any reason until it is finished. You cannot be interrupted while writing it—not even to greet a king, should one happen to stop by your cubicle. Some Reform rabbis hold that you are permitted to take one brief pause to check Twitter, if your mentions are really blowing up.

If you make a mistake, you may not erase it; instead, you must draw a line around the word to show that it is canceled, and the whole page must be put in a special burial place for Scripture (despite some similarities, this place is not the same as a bookstore). All of which is to suggest that perhaps you ought to consider going into another profession.

Over time, some Orthodox Jews began to feel that "Adonai" was itself too holy to say out loud, and began to favor "Hashem," or "The Name" in Hebrew. Then there are the names El, Eloah, Elohim, Elohai, El Shaddai, and Tzevao, all of which also mean things and have histories.

And this is to say nothing of the Ein Sof ("Endless")—a forty-two-letter name based on various permutations of YHWH—or the Shemhamphorasch, a seventy-two-letter name derived from three verses in Exodus that each contains seventy-two letters, which combine to form seventy-two names and can be used—by those with sufficient mystical knowledge—to ruin a perfectly good game of Scrabble. The *Sefer Yetzirah,* a book of the Kabbalah, even holds that the world was created through the manipulation of the sacred letters that form the names of G-d, whatever the hell that means.

Even English translations of the name are considered too holy to write. Thus, we render the words as "G-d," "L-rd," and even "The Alm-ghty." To be on the safe side, we also omit the vowels from such sentences as "Abe Vig-da's performance in *The G-dfather* was fucking brilliant."

WHAT ARE THE DIFFERENT TYPES OF JEWS?

Within the Jewish religion exist many subsets that, although the belief that there is but one G-d is consistent among all of them, approach ritual observance differently. Not unlike the way there are so many sects within Protestantism or so many different kinds of pizza.

Because their differences can range from substantial to subtle, probably the best way to illustrate them would be to establish a situation and then depict how members of each group would react.

So, let us say that it is Saturday, and lying on a sidewalk in front of a synagogue is a delicious broiled pork chop. And let's say, for the purposes of this example, that it is on a plate and there's no question whatsoever about its freshness and its obvious, straight-out-of-the-oven, untainted condition. Here is how, according to the tenets of their respective denominations, each type would behave.

Ultra-Orthodox—would walk past the pork chop because it is not kosher.

Hasidim—would put their arms over their heads and dance past the pork chop because it is not kosher.

Orthodox—would roundly boo the Hasidim because you are not allowed to dance on the Sabbath.

Humanistic—would smack the Orthodox because you are not allowed to roundly boo on the Sabbath.

Conservative—would remove their coat, place it over the pork chop, just stand there whistling some Israeli folk tunes for a few minutes, and then, when satisfied no one was looking, would pick up their coat with the pork chop hidden underneath, cut through neighbors' backyards, and sneak it into their detached garages because their homes are kosher.

Reconstructionist—would do all of the above except they'd actually eat the pork chop in their home before covering the house with a tent and moving into a motel for the month it was being fumigated.

Renewal—would pick up the pork chop, drive to a post office, and mail it to a Gentile friend.

Messianic—would pick up the pork chop with a pair of tongs, walk to the post office because you can't drive on the Sabbath, sleep in the post office lobby because you can't handle money to buy the stamps on the Sabbath, and then mail it to a Gentile friend on Monday morning when the post office reopens.

Reform—would make a beeline dash to Ikea, where they'd buy a table and a chair and then rush back and eat the pork chop right there on the sidewalk while going on dictionary.com to find out the meaning of the word "Sabbath."

It is our sincere hope that this clears up any confusion.

JEWISH NAMES

Names are very important in the Jewish tradition. It is said that the name given to an infant will determine that child's character. For example:

- The name "David" means "beloved," so a boy given that name will grow up to be popular.
- The name "Sarah" means "princess," so a girl given that name will have her own American Express Platinum card by age nine.
- The name "Alan" means "has an enormous head."

Ashkenazi Jews traditionally name babies after deceased relatives. So if you wanted to honor your beloved late uncle Shlomo, you would name your baby "Uncle Shlomo." In time she would get used to it.

In America, Jewish babies are often given both an English name and a Hebrew name. Babies who attend Faber College may also be given a Delta Tau Chi name such as "Flounder" by the late John Belushi.*

If you are a Jewish person who has a baby and have considered naming it, here's a chart of common biblical names and their meanings:

---

* Hebrew name: "Bluto."

COMMON BIBLICAL NAMES	MEANING
Aaron	Incontinent
Abby	On the husky side
Adam	Satan's dulcimer
Anthony	Bubble wrap
Barbara	Three nipples
Barney	Wash hands before returning to work
Benjamin	Broken headlight
Betty	Likes to bet
Bob	Smells like lox
Buck	Stops here
Calvin	Joint custody
Carl	Detached retina or butterfly
Charles	Allergic to mayonnaise
Claudia	Offside
Daniel	Clown school
Darnell	Turgid
Diana	The Empire State
Dick	Peter
Donald	Jockstrap of the Gods
Dorothy	Hedge clipper
Earl	Unkempt
Eliot	Da Do Ron Ron
Emily	Dances with wolves
Evan	Parking structure
Felice	Navidad
Fiona	Top of the morning
Franklin	Hard stool
Fred	Fredd
Frederick	Secure the perimeter
George	Kempt
Gina	Rotator of crops
Glen	Rectal itch
Glenn	Severe rectal itch
Gwen	Carving station

Harrison	Shake before using
Harvey	Celery
Herb	Herb (with a silent "h")
Hilda	Help, I've fallen and I can't get up
Hortense	Knee high to a grasshopper
Ike	Moves lips when reading
Irene	Our priest died
Isaac	Blessed angel or sump pump
Ivanka	Stain resistant
Jack	Roach infestation
Jennifer	Truncated
John	Born without spleen
Jonathan	Prefers window seat
Karl	Legume
Kenneth	May I have this dance? or pumpkin
Kris	Thunderdome
Lauren	Suspension bridge
Lawrence	Of Arabia
LeBron	Better than Jordan or Not as good as Jordan
Lima	A kind of bean
Luke	Hayseed or plutonium
Marcia	Cold sore
Marvin	Festering
Mary	*Capo de tutti capi*
Maureen	Honeycrisp apples
Melody	Harmony
Melvin	Corkage fee
Nancy	Visible panty line
Nelson	Heartbreak of psoriasis
Nina	Is literally chopped liver
Norbert	Nail polish remover
Norman	Gum disease
Oliver	Uncle Shlomo
Ophelia	Limit ten items

Oscar	Ingrown hair
Otto	Toot spelled inside-out
Paulette	Clockwise
Penelope	Not sold in stores
Peter	Dick
Queenie	Looks kind of like that girl in that movie
Quentin	Has a podcast
Quinn	Fraught
Richard	Self-cleaning oven
Rita	Dressing on the side
Robert	Skid mark
Roger	Cracked bathroom tile
Scott	Do not resuscitate
Shawn	Bus schedule
Steve	Loiters near Panera
Susan	Tourniquet
Teresa	Wears two pairs of underpants
Tom	Gelding
Tori	Arbor Day
Uncle Shlomo	Duke of Kent
Ursula	Warmonger or prune danish
Vanessa	Objects in mirror are closer than they appear
Veronica	MyPillow.com
Victor	Mold spore
Wally	Beaver's brother
Walter	Plummeting badger
Wanda	Bad Uber rating
Warren	Molten lava
Xavier	Costco member
Xena	Not a real name
Yves	Mole slayer
Yvonne	Gesundheit
Zeke	What in tarnation
Zelda	Pees in shower

THE BRIS

But first, the **Prelude to a Bris**.
   Ha ha.
   Sorry.

THE BRIS

The bris, or Brit Milah, is the ritual circumcision of a male Jewish infant on the eighth day of his life. It is one of three rituals that virtually all Jews observe, the other two being:

- The Bar/Bat Mitzvah.
- Eating at Chinese restaurants on Christmas.

Of course, in the United States circumcision is also common among non-Jews, but in their case the procedure is usually performed without fanfare by a physician in a medical facility while the parents cringe in another room. Whereas Jews make it into a big production, ordering food and inviting relatives and friends to come watch, as though the child were performing a violin recital instead of undergoing minor wiener surgery.

To the uninformed observer, Judaism's emphasis on foreskin removal may seem like a strange, even primitive obsession. In fact, however, there is a totally rational, scientific, medically sound reason why Jews do this: G-d told us to.

Not us *personally,* of course. This happened in biblical times, when G-d was always suddenly appearing before people and ordering them to perform bizarre tasks, like a divine version of *Survivor* host Jeff Probst. According to the Book of Genesis, G-d told Abraham, father of the Jewish people, that he and all his male descendants had to be circumcised, and Jews have been faithfully obeying G-d's will ever since, at least in this regard. We are less consistent about obeying G-d's will concerning, for example, shellfish.

The Brit Milah is traditionally conducted by a mohel—a person trained in performing the circumcision ritual. This is a serious and honorable profession, although unfortunately over the years it has become the subject of tasteless and immature humor in the form of crude jokes that we will not dignify by repeating, such as:

Q. What does a mohel say before performing the cut?
A. *"It won't be long now!"*

And:

Q. Why do waiters hate mohels?
A. *They never leave a tip.*

Ha ha! But in all seriousness, we are repulsed by these childish attempts at "humor" and many more like them that can be found on the internet.

In the Brit Milah ceremony, the baby is handed to the sandek, a godparent who has been seated in a chair to guard against the danger that he or she will keel over and fling the baby into the deli platter. The mohel then recites some blessings and performs the circumcision, during which he is required under Jewish law to draw some blood from the wound. Most mohels use a suction device to do this, but some Orthodox groups do it with their mouths and WHO ARE WE TO SAY THIS IS WEIRD AND CREEPY?

After the bris everybody enjoys a delicious meal, during which the infant's mother traditionally consumes roughly two liters of wine. The foreskin may either be buried or retained by the mohel for later use in the joke where he retires and has his collection of saved foreskins sewn together into a wallet, which when you rub it turns into a suitcase. Thank you, we'll be here all week.

GUIDELINE FOR NON-JEWS ATTENDING THEIR FIRST BRIS

1. Keep your mouth shut.

DISCUSSION QUESTIONS FOR "THE BRIS"

- Another crude mohel joke we will not dignify by speaking of it is the one with the punch line, "And every once in a while, they send back a giant prick like you."
- Who would not watch a movie called *Sendak, Sandek, What's the Difference?*, in which hilarity ensures when Maurice Sendak, the beloved author of *Where the Wild Things Are,* is mistaken for the sandek, whose job is to hold the baby being circumcised?

THE BAR/BAT MITZVAH

The Bar Mitzvah is a traditional ceremony held when a Jewish boy turns thirteen, to celebrate the fact that he has become a man in every sense of the word except the sense of reaching puberty, or having a job, or being able to lift anything heavier than a PlayStation controller. For girls the coming-of-age ceremony is called a Bat Mitzvah; in years past it was traditionally held when the girl turned twelve, but in modern times it takes place whenever her parents are able to get her to put down her iPhone.

The typical Bar/Bat Mitzvah service is held at a synagogue on a Saturday morning, starting about two hours before anybody outside the immediate family shows up. The "star of the show" is the new young adult, who leads the prayers and reads that week's passage from the Torah in Hebrew. At least it sounds like Hebrew. There is no way to know for sure.

After the reading the young adult traditionally makes a speech explaining how the Torah passage relates to modern life. This can be tricky if the passage is from, say, Leviticus, which, among other medical advice, contains detailed instructions on how a priest is supposed to treat skin diseases by (this is the actual procedure) killing a live clean bird over water in a clay pot, then dipping a *second* live clean bird into the first bird's blood and sprinkling it over the skin-disease victim seven times. One of the most inspirational parts of the Bar or Bat Mitzvah is watching a young Jewish adult take a Torah passage like this and heroically attempt to convert it into a Meaningful Life Lesson such as "Always help others."

The highlight of the service usually comes when the parents make their speeches. The format is for the parents to take turns addressing the young adult, repeatedly telling him or her, with great sincerity, that he or she is the most brilliant and talented individual the human race has ever produced. A child whose major life achievement is having reached eighth grade without burning down any major buildings will be hailed by the parents as a combination of Albert Einstein, Jonas Salk, Anne Frank, Sandy Koufax, Barbra Streisand, and Moses. It is a heavy burden of expectation to place on these young people, but most of them respond positively by going out into the world and not returning to the synagogue until they are in their late thirties.

HOSTING A BAR/BAT MITZVAH PARTY

The Bar/Bat Mitzvah party is an evening celebration traditionally hosted by the family of the Bar/Bat Mitzvah boy or girl after the luncheon buffet has been polished off. There has been some controversy surrounding these parties, with critics arguing that they have become too lavish, expensive, and "over the top," as exemplified by the now legendary 2016 Goldfarb Bar Mitzvah, for which the Goldfarbs rented the entire country of Guatemala for the evening and gave each guest, as a party favor, a new helicopter. Also, Tom Hanks made balloon animals, and the face-painting booth was manned by Jasper Johns.

Rest assured that there is no need for this kind of extravagance. The Bar/Bat Mitzvah is supposed to be a spiritual event; you do *not* have to spend millions of dollars on the party. In the words of the Conference of American Rabbinical Councils: "Eighty-five thousand dollars should be adequate, not including gratuities."

Here are the basic party requirements:

FOOD

Food is of course the most important element of any Jewish gathering, and we include lifeboat drills in that statement. But the Bar/Bat Mitzvah menu is especially critical. Remember: Some of your guests may not have had anything to eat for *nearly two hours*. So you will want to have plenty of food on hand. For example, if your entrée is prime rib, you should allow at least one head of cattle per family of four.

Bear in mind that your guests will be comparing the quality, quantity, and presentation of the food you serve to the quality, quantity, and presentation of the food they were served at other Bar/Bat Mitzvahs. If the Weintraub Bat Mitzvah had a dessert station featuring a life-size statue of Taylor Swift sculpted from chocolate, you need to respond with, at absolute minimum, Beyoncé. Remember: This is not a competition. This is a *war*.

MUSIC

Music should be provided by a professional DJ, defined as "a DJ with a sound system loud enough to liquefy concrete." The DJ should be assisted by a team of youthful, high-energy "party motivators" led by an upbeat microphone-wielding psychopath whose job is to sprint around the room incessantly hectoring the guests to MAKE SOME NOISE. A good rule of thumb is that if anybody within a radius of five hundred yards is able to carry on a coherent conversation, then your DJ team is not doing its job.

The party facilitators should lead the guests in traditional Jewish dances such as the Electric Slide. And, of course, everybody is required to join in for the fun and excitement of:

THE HORA

No Bar/Bat Mitzvah or Jewish wedding is complete without this dance, which symbolizes the ancient Jewish practice of rotating crops in a counterclockwise direction. At the first sounds of the song "Hava Nagila" (literally, "You Are Stepping on My Foot"), everybody forms a big circle, holds hands, and, following a deep-rooted cultural instinct, begins moving around the room with the natural grace and unison of a soccer riot.

The highlight of the hora comes when the Bar/Bat Mitzvah boy or girl and his or her family members are hoisted up on chairs and carried around. This tradition reminds us of a dark time in our history when Jews were not allowed into amusement parks, and thus had to simulate roller coasters by carrying each other around on furniture.

The chair tradition is a lot of fun, but it carries with it an element of physical risk; it should not be left to amateurs. According to the guidelines set forth by the Council of American Rabbinical Conferences, "Each chair should be hoisted aloft by four middle-aged, out-of-shape Jewish men who have been drinking." Also, when the person being hoisted is on the heavy side, the Council recommends that the hoisting be done "in the vicinity of one of the softer desserts, such as a large cheesecake, in case it is needed to cushion an emergency landing."

DISCUSSION QUESTIONS FOR
"THE BAR/BAT MITZVAH"

- You know the one about the Rubenstein family, who fly two hundred friends and relatives to southern India for their son Joshie's Bar Mitzvah, and after the service they put everybody on elephants to ride over to the party, and this incredible, mile-long parade of elephants is marching down the street, and everybody is feeling just wonderful, until all of a sudden the elephants stop moving, and they're just standing there, in the heat, for five minutes, ten minutes, and Mr. Rubenstein is getting more and more upset because he paid all this money to give his son the greatest Bar Mitzvah of all time, so finally he climbs down and walks over to the main elephant wrangler and demands to know what the holdup is, and the guy says "Please, Mr.

Rubenstein, be patient—there are four other Bar Mitzvahs ahead of us"?

- What does a sheep do when he turns thirteen? He has a Baaaa Mitzvah. One of the authors made that joke up when he was eight years old. His family still brings it up all the time. In fact, listening to them go on and on about it, you might well think it was the only funny thing he'd ever said.
- At what age should one permit a child to cash in the savings bonds he or she received as Bar/Bat Mitzvah gifts? What if he or she is cashing them in to fund a start-up company that he or she describes as "an app that's kind of like an Uber ride share, except you'll be able to pick your ride up along a fixed route at specific times," and does not seem to realize that he or she is attempting to invent the bus?

BAR/BAT MITZVAH Q&A FOR NON-JEWS

Q. We arrived at the synagogue at the hour shown on the invitation and there's hardly anybody here. Where is everybody?
A. *Jewish people generally avoid showing up too early for the Bar/Bat Mitzvah service, because they want to conserve their energy for the buffet.*

Q. There's a buffet?
A. *Of course. It's immediately after the service, and the buffet line can be a highly competitive environment requiring skill, stamina, and strength, especially if the lox starts to run low.*

Q. So when will the other guests arrive at the service?
A. *Veteran Bar/Bat Mitzvah attendees time their arrival for right around the throwing of the candy.*

Q. There's candy-throwing?
A. *Yes, toward the end of the service it's traditional to throw candy at the Bar/Bat Mitzvah boy or girl to symbolize the fact that it's time to eat already. Generally it's a soft jellied candy, but some people really hurl those things. If you're not careful you could lose an eye to an airborne Chuckle traveling upwards of seventy m.p.h. This is why the Rabbinical Council of America, in its official statement on this practice, says "you should shield your face with a prayer book."*

Q. If I'm a male, do I need to wear one of those little hats?
A. *What do you mean, "IF I'm a male"? You don't know?*

Q. I just meant . . .
A. *Relax! We are just kidding around. We Jews are known for our Jewish sense of humor.*

In all seriousness, that "little hat" is called a "yarmulke," or sometimes "gefilte fish," and Jewish men wear it inside the synagogue to symbolize the fact that they are Jewish men who are inside a synagogue. As a sign of respect you should wear one of the guest kippahs, which you will find just outside the synagogue in a box marked with this Hebrew lettering: אז הרה ראש.

Q. What does that mean?
A. *It means* WARNING: HEAD LICE.

No! We are still kidding! Such kidders we are! Just put on the little hat already.

Q. I notice that during the service different groups of people from the audience go up to the front and read something in strange singsong voices, and then everybody hugs everybody like they just won Final Jeopardy. What is that about?

A. These people are chanting in Hebrew from the Torah, a scroll of sacred text that is revered by the Jewish people because it was dictated by G-d directly to Moses, who wrote the entire thing down backward.

Q. Are the parts of the Torah that they're chanting inspirational passages relating to the Bar or Bat Mitzvah?
A. No. They could very well be chanting a three-thousand-year-old cure for skin disease.

Q. Ha ha! You're kidding again, right?
A. No.

Q. How can I tell when the service is over?
A. The service ends with the Aleinu, which is Hebrew for "stampede to the buffet."

FREQUENTLY ASKED QUESTIONS
ABOUT WHY YARMULKES ARE ROUND

Q. Why are yarmulkes round?

A. *Boy, you don't waste any time getting right to it, do you?*

Q. Well, isn't that the subject of this FAQ?

A. *True, but it doesn't leave any room for the history of the yarmulke or why men, and now a great many women, wear them during prayer or just in general.*

Q. I already know that stuff.

A. *In the form of a question, please.*

Q. Okay, why do I have to ask a question about something I already know the answer to?

A. *Atta boy!*

Q. . . . Well?

A. *Because others may not know that covering one's head is a sign of reverence. A way of honoring G-d . . .*

Q. Okay, now they know it. So why is it round?

A. *But few people know that yarmulkes weren't always round. That the early versions were actually rhomboids, which are oblique-angled parallelograms with only the opposite sides equal.*

Q. Why?

A. *Because in biblical times, largely due to the exertion it took to chew uncooked meat, men's heads tended to become lopsided and the rabbis felt that the rhombus would make for a better fit.*

Q. You've got to be kidding?

A. *No, but once mankind realized that fire had other uses in addition to lighting biblical farts, they started to cook beef and their heads slowly returned to a rounded form, thus rendering the rhombus (that's right, I just said "rendering the rhombus") impractical.*

Q. So that's when they changed the yarmulkes to be circular?

A. *No . . .*

Q. No?

A. *No, because the rabbis were so excited they were now eating meat that was tender because of the fires they cooked it over, they made the shape of yarmulkes to be exclamation points as an expression of their collective glee.*

Q. Exclamation points?

A. *Yep, a vertical-line yarmulke with a small circular yarmulke under it.*

Q. So men were, in effect, now wearing two yarmulkes?

A. *Yes. But once the initial jubilation at cooked meat wore off, the rabbis decided to rethink the vertical-line yarmulke.*

Q. Why?

A. *Because when the Philistines saw them they got really paranoid and said, "Who do you think you're pointing at?" and threatened to go to war. So the vertical-line yarmulke was done away with and the small circular part of the exclamation point was made bigger.*

Q. Hence, the shape of our current yarmulkes?

A. *You're a quick study.*

THE JEWISH WEDDING

The first recorded Jewish wedding took place more than thirty-eight hundred years ago, so at this point everybody who was directly involved is dead, although there is an ongoing dispute over the catering bill. This is only one way that the ancient wedding traditions of our Jewish ancestors are still very much alive today.

Another one is that usually at least one of the main participants in a Jewish wedding is Jewish. At one time there was a very strict rule that both bride and groom had to be Jewish, because that was the only way to ensure that nobody's mother would threaten to kill herself. Most strictly observant Jews still feel that they should marry within the faith, but in modern times there are large numbers of Jews who, although they identify themselves as Jewish, attend services roughly as often as they compete in the Kentucky

Derby. These people are more likely than previous generations to marry somebody of a different faith, but they often still want to incorporate some traditional Jewish elements into the wedding day, such as:

- The Tradition of the Two Families Becoming Embroiled in a Bitter Lifelong *G-dfather*-Level Grudge over the Reception Seating Chart
- The Tradition of Having a Carving Station with a Nice Prime Rib
- The Tradition of Serving the Salad Dressing on the Side
- The Tradition of Having a Table at the Reception Occupied by a Mystery Group of Alleged Relatives Whom Nobody in Either Family Can Positively Identify but Who Will Be on Their Third Helping of Prime Rib Before Other Tables Have Gotten Their First

There are also some important Jewish traditions involving the wedding ceremony itself. The main ones are:

THE KETUBAH

The ketubah is a signed contract between the bride and the groom spelling out their obligations in the marriage. It usually consists of two sections, one written in English and one in ancient Aramaic. Many people believe the English section is a translation of the Aramaic. These people are idiots. Here is a table summarizing the contents of the two sections:

WHAT THE ENGLISH SECTION SAYS
(WITH THE ARAMAIC TRANSLATION)

We are embarking on a great journey and the adventure of a lifetime.

Any violation of this contract is punishable by stoning.

We promise to love, honor, cherish, encourage, and inspire each other.

The bridegroom promises to pay the bride's family two hundred silver zuzim. Also to feed the bride.

Our hearts will fuse together as one to create a unique bond with passion and friendship at its core.

The bridegroom accepts the dowry provided by the bride's family, consisting of bedding, clothing, home furnishings, one large cooking vessel, two smaller cooking vessels, and six chickens, as having value of 115 silver zuzim.

We are soul mates and best friends and two crazy kids head over heels in love, and we have never been happier, and we seriously doubt that anybody ever has, even at the end of the movie *Bridget Jones's Diary* where Renée Zellweger and Colin Firth finally realize they are meant for each other and embrace in the snow-covered streets of London with her in her underpants. That was NOTHING compared to our happiness level.

Although the bridegroom wishes to have it noted for the record that one of the chickens appears to have dropsy.

We love each other SO MUCH, YOU GUYS.

The bridegroom agrees to engage in conjugal sex with the bride with a reasonable degree of frequency given the fact that she is not necessarily a looker compared to the bridegroom's various other brides.

When signing the ketubah, couples should bear in mind that everything in it is legally binding, which is why the American Conference of Rabbinical Councils strongly recommends that the bride and groom each engage the services of "a good ancient Aramean attorney."

THE CHUPPAH

The chuppah (pronounced "chutzpah") is a tentlike canopy under which the couple stands during a Jewish wedding ceremony. It symbolizes the tent of the biblical Abraham, who always kept his tent open on all sides because he wanted everybody to feel welcome, and also because the biblical diet tended to produce a lot of flatulence.

Many couples like to personalize their wedding chuppahs with iconic Jewish symbols or inspirational sayings such as GO JETS. Another Jewish tradition is that when a girl is born, her parents plant a cedar tree, and when a boy is born, his parents plant a cypress; when the girl and boy get married, their parents go to cut down the trees to make chuppah poles, but decide to use a rental chuppah instead, because what are they, lumberjacks?

THE CIRCLING

In olden days it was traditional for the bride in a Jewish wedding to circle the groom seven times, once for each dwarf. Many modern couples feel that this custom is outdated, and prefer a modified version in which the bride and the groom circle each other until one of them falls down, at which point the other is declared the winner. If there is a prenuptial agreement, sometimes the two lawyers will circle each other, then present the couple with invoices.

THE BREAKING OF THE GLASS

At the end of the ceremony, it is customary for the bridegroom to stomp on a lightbulb that has been wrapped inside a pillowcase or napkin. This reminds us of a time, thousands of years ago, when the Jewish people had no idea what to do with lightbulbs. At this point everybody shouts "Mazel tov!" (literally, "Watch out for shards!") and heads for the carving station.

Of course, this tradition, like the other wedding traditions and customs, can be modified according to the wishes of the bride and groom and their families. This is one of the hallmarks of Judaism: There is no one "right way" to do things. There are only many wrong ways.

JUDAISM AND INTERFAITH MARRIAGE

Let's begin with some troubling facts:

- More than half of all Jews in the United States marry outside the faith.
- For non-Orthodox Jews, the figure is more than 70 percent.
- The yamabiru, or Japanese mountain leech, which has five pairs of eyes and three jaws lined with thousands of tiny teeth, can *climb trees and drop down onto your head*.
- For every twenty adult Jews in the United States, there are now just seventeen Jewish children.

What do these facts mean to us, as Jews? They mean that if we go hiking in the mountains of Japan, we should wear a large hat. But they also mean that, if current trends continue, Judaism will eventually cease to exist altogether except in the form of bagels. This is why for many generations Jews considered interfaith marriage to be strictly taboo, like incest, or putting mayonnaise on corned beef.

The traditional antipathy of Jewish parents toward intermarriage was vividly dramatized in the hit Broadway play *Fiddler on the Roof,* which is about Tevye, a Jewish milkman in 1905 Russia who suffers from a Tourette's-like neurological disorder that causes him to blurt out weird unintelligible noises in the middle of his sentences, as in this example:

If I were a rich man daidle deedle daidle daidle daidle
deedle daidle dumb
All day long I'd biddy-biddy-bum

As you can imagine, this unfortunate condition has an adverse impact on Tevye's milkman career, as it seriously hampers his ability to interact with his customers:

CUSTOMER: I need two quarts of milk and one pint of cream.
TEVYE: Okay, that's two quarts of milk and one pint of boody booboo bimble beedle bom.
CUSTOMER: One pint of what?
TEVYE: Of bomby booby bomble binky bam bom g-ddammit shit.
CUSTOMER: Never mind.

So things are not going well financially for Tevye, and to make matters worse he has to support five daughters: Tzeitel, Hodel, Chava, Shprintze, and Beyoncé.

No, seriously, the fifth one is named Bielke. Tevye is eager to marry his daughters off, but when daughter Chava marries a Christian, Tevye refuses to speak to her ever again and tells the family to consider her dead. This seems pretty harsh, especially when you consider that Tevye is okay with his daughter Tzeitel marrying a man named "Motel." Granted, Motel is Jewish. *But his name is "Motel."*

The story ends on a bittersweet but hopeful note as Tevye, his wife, and their two youngest daughters prepare to leave their Russian village and travel to America, lured by the dream—shared by so many Jews of that era—of being as far away as possible from the Japanese mountain leech.

But the point is that in earlier times, almost all Jews strongly opposed marriage outside the faith. Many Jews still feel that way today, but intermarriage, especially in the United States, has become increasingly common. These interfaith couples face a number of important questions in the standard Q&A format.

Q. I am Jewish, and my spouse is Christian. Can we raise our children in both religions?
A. *Most experts recommend that, to avoid confusion and conflict, you choose one religion.*

Q. Scientology it is, then!
A. *NOT THAT ONE.*

Q. I have been told that if the father is Jewish, but the mother is not, the child is not considered Jewish.
A. *Who told you that?*

Q. Murray.
A. *Murray is an idiot.*

Q. What other scary creatures are found in Japan?
A. *There's the Japanese giant hornet, which is the size of a commuter aircraft, but more venomous.*

Q. Jesus Christ! Speaking of whom: We're an interfaith couple who've decided to raise our children in the Jewish faith. Can we still have a Christmas tree?
A. *We asked the American Rabbinical Council of Rabbis in America, and their answer was: "As long as you do not pay retail for it."*

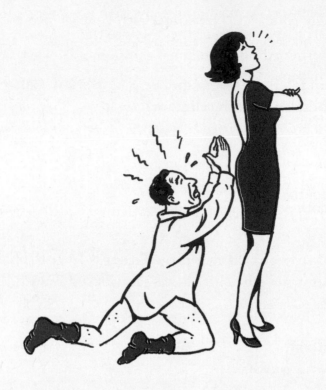

JUDAISM AND SEXUALITY

In many major religions—we will not name names, except to say
that one of them rhymes with "Fristianity"—sex is viewed as sinful.
These religions believe that sex is not supposed to be enjoyable; the
only acceptable reason for engaging in it is to procreate. Sex is seen
as a necessary biological activity, like pooping, except that instead
of poop you produce babies. These religions have given sex a bad
name. (Specifically, "sex.")

In stark contrast, the official stance of Judaism is that sex is
great. Judaism views sex as a holy act. Seriously: that is the *official
stance.* This is one of the best features of Judaism. Sure, we don't
have Fristmas, with all the presents and festive parties and Fristmas
carols and Fanta Flaus, but WE HAVE SEX. In fact, according to
Jewish law, we are *required* to have sex. A LOT. The Talmud actually

lays out (ha!) specifically how often a man is supposed to have sex with his wife. According to the Talmud, the frequency of marital sex is determined by the man's profession, as follows (we are not making this up):

- Independently wealthy men: once a day
- Laborers: twice a week
- Donkey drivers: once a week
- Camel drivers: once every thirty days
- Sailors: once every six months

We are a little unclear on the Talmud's reasoning here. We understand why sailors can't have frequent marital sex: they're out at sea. But why would camel drivers be expected to have sex with their wives less frequently than donkey drivers? Do camel drivers smell worse? Is it because they're having sex on the side with their camels? Far be it from us to speculate.

What *is* clear is that the Talmud believes that laborers, who are tired from doing hard productive work, are expected to have sex with their wives less often than men of independent means, who don't engage in any activity more strenuous than lining up putts. To put it in mathematical terms, the amount of sex a Jewish man is expected to have with his wife is inversely proportional to the amount of productive physical work he does.

Of course, in modern times we have far fewer camel and donkey drivers, thanks to Uber. On the other hand, we have many new professions that the authors of the Talmud could never have imagined, such as astronaut and Kardashian. So as a guide for modern Jewish men who wish to engage in marital sex with the correct frequency, we have updated the Talmudic requirements for various professions, based on the amount of productive physical labor involved:

JEWISH MAN'S PROFESSION	FREQUENCY WITH WHICH HE HAS SEX WITH HIS WIFE
Lumberjack, construction worker, truck driver, auto mechanic, fisherman, coal miner:	*Jewish men do not do these things.*
Bitcoin miner:	*We have no idea what this means, so we're going with twice a week.*
Professional athlete:	*Again, we are talking about Jewish men.*
Lawyer, physician, dentist, accountant, executive:	*Every other day*
Anything involving social media:	*Daily*
Venture capitalist:	*Five times a day*
Mark Zuckerberg:	*Thirty-seven times a day*

At this point you are wondering: "Why is this all about the husbands? Don't the wives have any say in this matter?"

Yes, they do. In fact, Judaism has always been very enlightened on the issue of female sexuality. The Talmud says that Jewish wives do not have to have sex with their husbands if they don't feel like it, which they often don't, according to many traditional jokes, such as:

Q. What is Jewish foreplay?
A. *Three hours of begging.*

Q. Why do Jewish women like Chinese food?
A. *Because "won ton" spelled backward is "not now."*

Of course, these are just jokes; in fact, Jewish women love to have sex with their husbands whenever the mood strikes them, which is roughly every other Arbor Day.

Ha ha! We are just kidding.*

We must caution that, although Judaism is strongly pro-sex, this does not mean that "anything goes." By a strict traditional interpretation of the Talmud, certain sexual acts are considered "non-kosher," including extramarital sex, masturbation, and sex with shellfish. Also, strictly observant married couples are not supposed to have sex during certain Times of the Month, if you follow our drift.

Of course, in modern times, many Jews take a broader view of what kinds of sexual activity are permissible. The important thing, as you make your own decisions on these matters, is to view sex as an act of love, not just indiscriminate passion, and to be sensitive to the needs of your partner. So it should be a consenting shellfish.

* We are not really kidding.

SODOM AND GOMORRAH

With the possible exception of "Twist and Shout," no two words are said together more often than "Sodom and Gomorrah"—biblical cities along the Jordan River whose people engaged in such deviant behavior and impenitent sin that G-d felt He had no choice but to destroy them both.

What kind of deviant behavior? Well, let's start with the fact that the term "sodomy" (which pertains to "sexual crimes against nature" like oral and anal) is derived from "Sodom." Or that "gomorrahification" (which pertains to the even more heinous sexual crimes like nasal, occipital, and glacial) is derived from "Gomorrah."*

So, despite emphatic warnings to Lot, a righteous resident in whom G-d confided and to whom G-d appealed to have those residents change their ways, G-d ultimately opted to make an example of these decadent cities by ravaging them with fire and brimstone—a form of sulfur that hardens objects after they cool off. Such was the fate of Lot's wife, who, after being told not to look back at the flaming cities they were fleeing, defied the Lord's wishes, looked back, and was immediately turned into a pillar of salt, upon which Lot and his descendants rolled ears of buttered corn at Old Testament picnics for generations to come.

---

* While archaeological excavations of the nearby town of Dildo have uncovered elongated chunks of brimstone, the lack of consensus among the rabbis as to whether they were used for sexual pleasure or as primitive toilet paper holders have denied Dildo's place in infamy alongside Sodom and Gomorrah.

JEWISH DIVORCE

In biblical times, it was easy for a Jewish man to divorce his wife. Basically, all he had to do was hand her a document—called a "get"—stating that he was divorcing her. He could do this for pretty much any reason, including excessive flatulence. That's right: the husband could simply *hand his wife a piece of paper,* whenever he felt like it, and just like that, bada bing, bada boom, she was his ex-wife. Whereas Jewish women had essentially no rights at all. So it was pretty sweet.

No, wait, we mean it was NOT pretty sweet. It was very bad. It was an evil discriminatory sexist system in which an oppressive patriarchy employed masculine hegemony to subjugate women and persons of gender, and the authors of this book totally do not agree with it. We favor the modern view of divorce, under which a marriage is a contract between two equal individuals that cannot be dissolved without many thousands of dollars in attorneys' fees racked up over months, if not years, of bitter legal wrangling over such matters as who gets the Jet Ski.

Nevertheless, many traditional Jewish communities still observe biblical divorce traditions. This means that, in addition to the requirements of civil law, women in these communities must be given a get by their husbands in order to be considered truly divorced. This can be problematic, because some husbands, for revenge or other motives, refuse to grant the get, which means their wives cannot remarry. Sometimes these women, or their families, employ strong measures to persuade the husbands to change their minds, as was dramatized in an episode of—speaking of bada bing—*The Sopranos,* in which Tony Soprano, having been asked by an Orthodox Jewish business associate to persuade his daughter's extremely stubborn husband to grant her a get, succeeds by threatening to castrate the husband with bolt cutters.

Of course, that was a fictional, dramatized, grossly exaggerated depiction that does not in any way reflect real life. In real life, Tony would follow the guidance of the Association of Associated American Rabbinical Councils of America, which recommends, quote, "hedge shears with blades measuring a minimum of ten inches."

CONVERTING TO JUDAISM

People convert to Judaism for many reasons: they want to marry a Jewish person whose mother has mentioned that she will swallow rat poison if her child marries a non-Jew; they're tired of paying retail; they're unpopular and would like to be able to blame it on anti-Semitism; they have heard that Jews are intelligent and they would like to be intelligent; they were devout Christians but got subjected to the song "The Little Drummer Boy" one too many times at the mall and on the thirty-seven-hundredth repetition of "rump-pa-pum-pum" they snapped. . . . The list goes on and on. Some people even convert to Judaism because they actually agree with the core beliefs of Judaism, although nobody seems to know what they are.

Whatever the reason, every year a number of people—and we fully intend to look that number up on the internet before this book is published—convert to Judaism. Perhaps you are considering converting. If so, you probably have some questions that you would like to see answered below in the Q&A format.

Q. Do I have to get circumcised?
A. *Yes.*

Q. But I'm a woman.
A. *The rules are the rules.*

Q. What if I'm a man who has already been circumcised?
A. *You'll have to be circumcised again.*

Q. How does that work?
A. *Don't ask. It involves finding an eyelid donor.*

Q. Are there any other requirements for conversion?
A. *You must pass a physical test, which includes tearing a four-day-old loaf of challah in half barehanded and completing both the two-hundred-meter Torah Carry and the 150-decibel Shofar Blow. Also, you and three other conversion candidates must lift and hold aloft for one minute a chair containing a simulated groom weighing 225 pounds. If you're converting to Orthodox Judaism, you'll also need to complete the forty-year Wilderness Wander.*

Q. Do I have to know Hebrew?
A. *You don't have to be fluent in Hebrew, but it's a good idea to learn some basic phrases, such as* shalom *("aloha"),* gesundheit *("you got mucus on my garment"), and* kol hakavod *("our doorman is an albino").*

Q. Is there some kind of final exam?
A. *Yes. Once you have completed your training, you will appear before a religious court consisting of three rabbis—called a beth din—where you will be expected to discuss the core beliefs of Judaism.*

Q. What are they?
A. *The rabbis are hoping you can tell them.*

THE JEWISH HOME

Jewish homes are typically quite similar to other homes in the same neighborhood except for a smear of lamb's blood on the front door, just in case. Careful observers might note other differences, too. For example, a Jewish home will not have a pig roasting on a spit in the backyard, a giant portrait of Jesus, or a giant portrait of anybody. There will probably not be any camping equipment, either. Some Jewish homes do not even have Christmas trees. But a Jewish home does have several distinctive features:

Two People Carrying on a Conversation or Argument Despite Being in Different Rooms of the House. Depending on the size of the house and family, multiple conversations/arguments may be happening simultaneously, but no two participants will be in the same room.

A Person Reading a Book on the Toilet Because It Is the Only Place He Can Get Some Peace and Quiet. They could also be reading a magazine. In fact, the Jews have their own magazine. It is called *The New Yorker*.

Mezuzahs. Deuteronomy 6 says that Jews should post the words of the Sh'ma on the doorposts of their homes, which is peculiar in that Jews believe Deuteronomy was written in the time of Moses, when doorposts were not exactly a major part of Jewish domestic life. A mezuzah is a small container that holds the parchment on which the Sh'ma is written, but in a typical feat of Jewish business savvy, *you have to buy the parchment separately*. If you want a *kosher* parchment handwritten by a trained scribe, well, that's gonna run you extra.

If it surprises you to learn that there have been years of intense rabbinical debate about how to hang a mezuzah, you are not much for paying attention. Naturally, some rabbis held that a mezuzah must be vertical, while others advocated vehemently for horizontality. But unlike the other 5,455,231,998 instances of rabbinical disagreement, this one has been resolved: the rabbis concluded that a mezuzah should hang at a forty-five-degree angle, inclined inward, to ward off declining property values.

Ketubah. Many Jews frame or thumbtack up their ketubah, a traditional marriage contract written in Aramaic, the technical legal language of Talmudic law. This might seem sweet and romantic, unless you can read Aramaic,* in which case you would realize that what is hanging on your wall is an ice-cold prenup spelling out exactly who has to do what for this to work and who gets what if it doesn't.

An Unread Paperback Copy of the Novel *Exodus* by Leon Uris. Depending on the household, this may have been inherited from parents or grandparents, who also never read it.

---

* You can't.

KEEPING KOSHER

Everyone* has a theory about the origins of kashruth, the system of Jewish dietary laws that makes the U.S. tax code look both simple and reasonable.

Some people argue that Hashem created kashruth to keep us healthy: if you eat an undercooked pig, you can catch a scorching case of trichinosis and poop yourself to death, so it's better to avoid eating pigs at all. Others argue that this is extremely stupid, because an undercooked chicken can also kill you, and we're allowed to eat chickens. Besides which, if Hashem was so concerned with our health, why not just make us immune to pig-borne illnesses? Also, why allow the Jews to eat other truly disgusting foods, such as

* Not *everyone* everyone, but everyone.

tongue sandwiches and cholent, a stew that is frequently mistaken for an industrial waste product?

Another theory is that kashruth was intended to strengthen our identity as a people and separate us from neighboring tribes* by causing them to be annoyed whenever they invited us over for dinner until eventually they just stopped, the way you have no doubt done with the vegans in your life. But if this were true, why did Hashem not simply afflict all of us—rather than a mere 60 percent—with lactose intolerance?

Yet another theory is that the specific, esoteric, idiosyncratic, arbitrary, and downright bizarre rules of kashruth are less important than the *idea* of obsessively following a set of specific, esoteric, idiosyncratic, arbitrary, and downright bizarre rules. In other words, the answer is *Because*.

THE BASIC LAWS OF KASHRUTH

- Animals with cloven hooves (cows, sheep, goats, deer, stoats, marmots, mozzarella buffaloes, brontosauri) that chew their cud are kosher.
- Nobody knows what cud is, including these animals.
- All other mammals are *trayf,* from the Hebrew word *terafya,* meaning "delicious," and are not to be eaten or even looked at with hungerous intent. This includes pigs, camels, hyenas, bunny rabbits, sloths, horsies, koalas, varmints, flying squirrels, and duck-billed platypi. Nor are any products derived from them kosher. This includes many glues (which contain horse hooves), gummy bears (gelatine; bears), hard cheeses (rennet, which comes from the stomach lining of Presbyterian sheep), and suits made of pig leather.

---

* Such as the Amirites, Amiwrongs, Assyrians, Hittites, Demerols, Orcs, and Called Quests.

- Animals must be slaughtered in a humane manner, by a trained assassin, with a single stroke of a blade with no nicks in it. Though in a pinch, a mohel is also fine.
- Certain parts of approved animals slaughtered according to kashruth law still aren't kosher, because Jews are not permitted to eat the sciatic nerve found in the hindquarters (or "ass") of certain animals. This eliminates such choice cuts as filet mignon, sirloin steak, London broil, and leg of lamb, which is why they are primarily served at clubs that do not accept us as members.
- Seafood is kosher if it has fins and scales. You know what has fins and scales? All the most boring fish in the ocean. The fish nobody invites to cocktail parties, much less serves with cocktail sauce. You know what doesn't have fins and scales? Yeah, of course you do. We're not even going to write it all out, because it's too depressing.
- All food served at Chinese restaurants is kosher, including pork, shellfish, and the glue used in manufacturing takeout containers. You can also rock a cheeseburger and a milk shake in the parking lot of a Chinese restaurant and it's fine. You can even get high on methamphetamines and kill somebody. Chinese restaurants are a 100 percent free zone.
- Domesticated fowl—geese, turkeys, ducks, chickens, turduckens, pheasants, those owls from *Harry Potter*—are kosher, but birds of prey (eagles, hawks, those birds from *The Birds,* unusually aggressive titwillows) are *trayf.* Rabbis are divided on whether you're allowed to train a falcon for years, then turn on it and eat it, but they agree that it's probably not worth it.
- But wait, there's more! Blood is also *trayf,* so the tough, undesirable cuts left of the cud-chewing, cloven-hoofed animals butchered by the specially trained shohet have to be *kashered* by draining the blood and then washing and salting the meat. Also, just to be safe, you have to cook the leftover

hunks of meat until they are basically smoldering lumps of carbon. Or you could just become a vegetarian.

- The Bible says you're not supposed to cook an animal in its mother's milk, because "that's super effed-up." But that wasn't restrictive enough for the rabbis, so they decided you couldn't mix meat and dairy at all, or even use the same plates for them. The Jews were like, "Man, lucky thing chickens don't give milk, amirite?" So the rabbis extended the rule to include fowl. After that the Jews, wisely, did not bring up fish.

- Neutral, or "pareve," foods can be eaten with either meat or dairy. These would be your grains, fruits, Chili Cheese Fritos, Pop-Tarts, vegetables, Krab brand fake crabmeat, trail mix, LSD, and gelatine-free gummy bears.

- Wine and other products made from grapes (juice, jelly, John Steinbeck's classic novel *Of Mice and Men*) must be monitored and authorized as kosher by a rabbi. Fun fact: "wine monitor" is the job 99 percent of rabbis go to rabbinical school in the hopes of getting.

SELTZER

Seltzer, the Yiddish word for Pellegrino, is a beverage whose origin dates back to our days in ancient Egypt when, after a hard day of slavery, Jews returned home with a profound thirst for tasteless soda water.

However, since such a drink did not yet exist, their desires went unquenched and their anguished cries of "This water is flat!" and "Who do I have to sleep with to get a few bubbles!" were more plaintive than any of the ones heard during their ruthless daily lashings.

This frustration lasted throughout their bondage until one Shabbat night at Moses's house when Jacob's family came over for dinner and his youngest son, Fizz, accidentally fell into the trough that Moses's pet paschal lamb drank from. While thrashing about in his attempt to save himself, the rather portly lad's submerged exhaling infused the water with extraordinary amounts of carbon dioxide. Then, after pulling the upended tyke out of the water, Moses and Jacob couldn't help noticing it now had an effervescence that caused the paschal lamb to belch after imbibing. Eager with anticipation, they then dared to dip their kiddush goblets into the bubbly liquid, took a sip, smiled triumphantly, and wisely decided that Jacob should be the designated chariot driver when they went home, as his wife, Leah, was drinking wine with her delicious dinner.

Consequently, because people in the Old Testament lived incredibly long lives, Jews enjoyed what was now being called seltzer for the next 679 years as Fizz made a virtual fortune going from home to home hurling himself into people's troughs, bathtubs, and those large aquariums found in the waiting rooms of biblical dentists' offices.

And seltzer did not die upon Fizz's death. For as knowledge of carbonation became widespread, it endured throughout European history (it is said that in 1215 King John of England received a congratulatory case of seltzer from Archbishop Langton after signing the Magna Carta). It found its way to the New World during the early twentieth century and was delivered to homes and dispensed from soda fountains, where it became known as "Two Cents Plain" in deference to the fact that it had no flavor—until President Franklin Roosevelt began bathing in it with hopes of its curing his paralysis, at which point it was bottled and sold as men's aftershave called "Essence of Franklin," which was, despite FDR's popularity, not commercially successful.

TZEDAKAH

The Hebrew word "tzedakah" literally means "justice" or "righteousness," though it is commonly used to signify "charity"—pretty much the same way the English word "trump" literally means "outdo" though it is also commonly used to mean "huge turd who is a blight on our democracy and an abject embarrassment in front of the entire world."

Unlike the Western concept of charity, which is viewed as the voluntary and somewhat spontaneous practice of giving to the less fortunate, tzedakah is more of an ethical obligation that *must* be performed despite one's financial standing. Thus, setting aside a portion (usually 10 percent) of one's income or of a farmer's crops for the needy is known as a *tithe* and is regarded as one of the three acts that can offset an otherwise unfavorable heavenly decree—the

other two being not cheating on your taxes and not pointing to another person after you've silently passed wind on a crowded elevator.

This practice was explained in great detail by Moses Maimonides (1135–1204), who was a Jewish philosopher and one of the most
prolific writers and Torah scholars of his or any century. In addition
to being a rabbi, Maimonides (aka Rambam, aka Overachiever) was
a noted physician and astronomer who elaborated on the eight levels of tzedakah in his fourteen-volume *Mishneh Torah,* which is now
available in both paperback and eBook but has a surprisingly low
sales ranking despite blurbs by Professor Alan Dershowitz and rap-
per Ice-T on the book jacket.

In the *Mishneh Torah,* Maimonides lists the eight levels of giving,
which are:

1. Giving an interest-free loan or a job to a person in need so
    he no longer has to live by relying on others—except when
    it comes to a goldbrick in-law who will keep trying to drain
    you dry no matter how much you do for him.
2. Giving tzedakah anonymously to a known recipient—
    except when it comes to that same in-law, so you can now
    point to the rest of the extended family and say, "Hey, I
    gave already! How about someone else chipping in for a
    change?"
3. Giving tzedakah anonymously to an unknown recipient—
    although the *Mishneh Torah* says nothing about not
    including your Instagram handle so he can publicly thank
    you if and when he gets a phone.
4. Giving tzedakah publicly to an unknown recipient—as
    in, "Hey, you who's selling pencils on those subway steps.
    Would you like a job as my dental hygienist?" And while
    we're supposed to give charity with no expectation of
    anything in return, someone who overheard you could very
    well offer you his or her seat on the train because of your
    graciousness.

5. Giving tzedakah before being asked—especially to a person whom you're positive will eventually ask you for money or a ride to the airport during the Super Bowl. This just saves a lot of precious time.

6. Giving tzedakah after being asked—see level number 5.

7. Giving willingly, but inadequately. We're pretty sure this also includes begrudgingly.

8. Giving out of pity as opposed to giving because it's a religious obligation. This seems to be the most important reason and we're baffled as to why it's the lowest level on this list. As a result, the authors of this book firmly feel that Maimonides, though dead for over eight hundred years, still has a little work to do on his personal growth.

DEATH

Death is the end of life as we know it. All things, with the possible exception of reruns of *Seinfeld,* are going to stop existing one day. Exactly what happens to us when we pass away is probably the most asked question in all religions.

But how do Jews feel about the subject? Do we believe in heaven? Hell? Are we ever going to see our deceased loved ones again and, if so, will some of them irritate us as much as they did when they were alive? To fully understand how our people regard this phenomenon, it's important to start at the very beginning.

THE HISTORY OF DEATH

While it's very possible that some fish, birds, and animals died beforehand, the first human death occurred in the Garden of Eden when Adam and Eve's son, Cain, killed their other son, Abel. And though the Old Testament is unclear as to the exact method Cain used to off his brother, it is quite specific as to his parents' reaction when they saw Abel lying inert on the ground.

ADAM

What's with Abel?

EVE

I have no idea. He hasn't said a word or moved a muscle for a few days now.

ADAM

What should we do with him?

EVE

I'm not sure.

ADAM

You okay?

EVE

I'm starting to grieve.

ADAM

What's that mean?

EVE

I'm not sure. But I feel sad.

Over the following centuries, as more and more people were born and more and more of those people died, the Jewish people developed their own set of beliefs and rituals as to what to do once a person stops living.

PREPARING THE BODY

Once it's determined that a body is indeed dead, it is then washed and wrapped in a shroud as if to dress the deceased for his entrance into the next world. What if the deceased had already showered in the morning of the day he died? And what if that squeaky-clean dead person just so happened to be wearing a shroud that day? The rabbis agree that as a way of thanking the deceased for relieving some unfortunate person of the icky task of washing and dressing a dead body, a five-dollar food voucher should be buried with the dearly departed, just in case there's an In-N-Out Burger in heaven. As a rule, Orthodox Jews assign someone to sit vigil with the body the night before the funeral to keep company with the deceased's soul before it leaves the body and, on a more mundane level, to make sure that no one breaks in and steals that five-dollar food voucher.

THE FUNERAL

Jews bury quickly. While other religions tend to wait upwards of a week to have a funeral, we often start making arrangements if a person merely oversleeps.

Upon entering the funeral home, the immediate family observes the rite of *k'riah,* which is making a small rip in an article of clothing as a symbol of grief. And because it's considered an archaic custom to physically rend one's actual shirt, blouse, pants, or sports jacket with their bare hands, nowadays most mourners merely have a black ribbon pinned to them that is then slit by a scissor or razor blade.

This is not only a less dramatic display of bereavement but has also proved to be a huge windfall for anyone who had the foresight to invest in black ribbon, scissor, or razor blade stocks.

Because life is considered to be a gift from G-d, the funeral service, including the prayer for the dead called Kaddish, is not a lament for the departed but rather a glorification of G-d and an expression of thanks for giving this person life in the first place. Therefore, the friends and relatives who choose to speak are encouraged to recount humorous anecdotes that will make the assembled rejoice in the memories that both are life affirming and will help assuage their grief. Then again, if the deceased never did or said anything humorous or was, in fact, a misanthrope who didn't enjoy any aspect of his or her life, then it's very possible that the dead person is happy that he or she is dead so no one needs cheering up and it's a win-win for everyone.

THE BURIAL

Because "Ashes to ashes and dust to dust" is a tenet that Jewish people embrace, we bury our dead in a plain pine casket with wooden screws so everything will eventually decay and there'll be nothing left, especially if the deceased's bones and teeth happened to be made of ashes and dust.

At the cemetery, after the burial service has been completed, mourners are invited to take turns grabbing a shovel, turning it over so its rounded underside is facing upward, scooping dirt from a pile, and depositing dirt onto the already lowered casket. The reason we use the bottom part of the shovel is to symbolize how reluctant we are to do what we're doing—similar to the way a guest at a dinner party will surreptitiously turn his spoon upside down to make believe he's eating the disgusting soup he's been served or how a postcoital lover will invert his or her body when their partner says, "Spoon me" during a regrettable one-night stand.

OBSERVING THE MOURNING PERIOD

After the burial, the immediate family of the departed returns home to begin the mourning period called shiva. Shiva literally means "seven" and refers to the weeklong period during which mourners cover their mirrors, sit on uncomfortable wooden benches, and refrain from working, shaving, having sex, or doing anything joyous. This is to eschew our own vanity so we can maintain focus on the departed, who, although decaying six feet underground, is probably having a better time than the mourners at this point. Most Jews today sit shiva for only three days while making a mental note to lie and say that they sat for all seven days should they eventually run into the departed up in heaven.

THE EVIL EYE

The evil eye—in Hebrew, *ayin ha'ra*—is the power to cause harm to others merely by looking at them. Although the evil eye is mentioned multiple times in the Torah and the Midrash, some people dismiss it as superstitious nonsense. The vast majority of these people are dead within hours.

Because the truth is that the evil eye is real. How do we know this? We know this because in the waning seconds of an NBA game in the 1980s between the Boston Celtics and the Philadelphia 76ers, Larry Bird miraculously missed *two crucial free throws in a row,* thereby opening the door for the Sixers to win the game. The only possible explanation for this is that Bird was being stared at with malicious intent from close range by one of the authors of this book and his friend Buzz Burger.

So please do not speak to us of superstition.

Is there any way to protect yourself from the evil eye? Yes, there is. Here is a direct quote from the Talmud, which we are not making up:

One who enters a city and fears the evil eye should hold the thumb of his right hand in his left hand and the thumb of his left hand in his right hand and recite the following: I, so-and-so son of so-and-so, come from the descendants of Joseph, over whom the evil eye has no dominion.

At this point you are thinking: If it's that simple, why didn't Larry Bird do it? We have asked ourselves that very question countless times over the years, and the only answer we can come up with is: poor scouting.

Another common technique for warding off the evil eye is to wear hamsas, which are rodents belonging to the subfamily *Cricetinae.*

No, sorry, those are hams*ters,* which are generally ineffective against the evil eye and should not be worn as warding devices except in an emergency. We meant *hamsas,* which are amulets shaped like a hand with an eyeball in the palm, although it is usually not a real eyeball. Scholars tell us that the *hamsa* is an ancient symbol representing a hand that for some reason has an eyeball in it. Thanks, scholars!

Another technique for warding off the evil eye is to spit three times, but bear in mind that—in the words of Rabbi Shmuel Kornblatt (1704–1953)—"you will definitely draw a technical foul."

THE AFTERLIFE

The only thing Jews agree on, when it comes to the afterlife, is that it's not something to spend too much time worrying about. This may seem surprising, given our propensity to worry about everything, but worrying about what happens after we die could eat up a lot of hours, leaving us scrambling to find sufficient time to worry about the present and the earthly future—and if that doesn't fill you with anxiety, then frankly we are a bit worried about your commitment to worrying.

Beyond that, Jews are all over the map.* Some of us believe that the souls of the dead are transported to heaven, and the souls of the not-so-awesome to a kind of purgatory realm called Gehinnom,

---

* This is not what led Henry Ford to coin the term "International Jewry."

She'ol, or the Department of Motor Vehicles, where they spend a year being tormented by the personal demons they created with each sin, joining the righteous in heaven thereafter.

Others, including many Hasidic sects, believe that a soul is reincarnated through many lifetimes—which also offers an elegant explanation for the mystical belief that every Jew who has ever lived was spiritually present at Mount Sinai and agreed to the covenant with G-d, particularly if one is not very good at math—or that wicked souls are not rehabilitated but simply destroyed, or that the dead stay dead until the Messiah comes, at which time the good eggs are resurrected into eternal life, though some also believe that they die a second physical death, only to be brought back a third time in heaven. And still others of us believe that this is all a load of horseshit and once you're dead you're worm food and that's that.

The World to Come in the afterlife is known as Olam Ha-Ba, though this term also refers to the messianic age. Both the Mishnah and the Talmud make reference to the idea that the afterlife is the one that counts, comparing our world to a lobby and the Olam Ha-Ba to a banquet hall and suggesting that the World to Come is like the Sabbath and this lifetime like the eve of the Sabbath, a time of preparation and baking large chickens.

All of which makes it even more remarkable that the great scholars are also like, "Eh, but don't give it too much thought." But this is because a Jew is supposed to perform mitzvoth (good deeds) for their own sake, not in anticipation of some cushy afterlife reward. Otherwise, that Jew is no better than a disobedient child who falls in line because he doesn't want to miss out on dessert. Or a Christian.

The Talmud does contain statements that a particular good deed will guarantee a person's place in the Olam Ha-Ba, or that a particular sin will cause that place to be forfeited. But—and you gotta love this—these statements are considered by most scholars to be nothing more than hyperbole. Can you name another religion in which the main advice about how to gain entry to paradise is generally dismissed as just a bunch of shit-talk? Go ahead, we'll wait.

So what is the realm of Gan Eden like? Some rabbis have said that the peace one feels in properly experiencing Shabbat is a mere one-sixtieth of the peace one feels in Gan Eden. This is all the more remarkable because the rabbis in question reached this conclusion without using a calculator. Other classic wisenheimer-rabbi descriptions of the afterlife include the one about how Moses lectures all day on the Torah, which is heaven for the righteous and hell for the schmucks, and the one about how in the afterlife nobody can bend their elbows, so the righteous feed each other and the wicked use the vast fortunes they amassed during their earthly lives in mergers and acquisitions to hire personal feeders.

THE
JEWISH
YEAR

THE JEWISH CALENDAR

At first glance the Jewish calendar may seem confusing, but in fact it can be easily understood by anyone with a master's degree in astronomy and at least eight years of rabbinical training.

The "building blocks" of the calendar are the twelve Hebrew months. The easiest way to learn them is to memorize this traditional Jewish children's song:

First comes Nisan, it's month number one
When it ends that means the month of Iyar has begun
With Sivan coming right behind
But also keep Tammuz, Av, Elul, and Tishrei in mind
Then Cheshvan, Kislev, Tevet, Shevat, and Adar come along

And that is how we remember the names of the twelve months in the Jewish calendar in the form of a traditional song!

In the old days Jewish children would recite this song every night until they were old enough to run away. However, in modern times, many Jewish parents do not have time to pass along this kind of traditional knowledge because of other demands on their time, specifically Netflix. Thus, today many Jews are more familiar with the Gregorian (or "regular") calendar, which is based solely on the sun, as opposed to the Jewish calendar, which is based on a combination of the lunar cycle, the solar cycle, and the mating cycle of the Atlantic herring.

Unlike Gregorian months, the Jewish months are each equal to one lunar cycle, or twenty-eight and a half days. This means the twelve Jewish months add up to only 354 days, which is eleven days short of the 365-day solar cycle. If this difference were left uncorrected, Jewish people would fall behind by eleven days every year, and their president would still be Harry Truman. But there would also be some negative consequences, which is why an extra "leap" month is added to the Jewish calendar seven times every nineteen years, during the third, sixth, eighth, eleventh, fourteenth, seventeenth, and nineteenth years. Seriously.

This eleven-day difference in calendar years is the reason why the dates of Jewish holidays appear to "jump around" when compared to Christian holidays such as Christmas and the Fourth of July. Even Jews are often unsure of the timing of Jewish holidays, which are constantly springing up out of nowhere and taking people by surprise, like ancient festival versions of Freddy Krueger.

But if the Jewish calendar is confusing to Jews, imagine how incomprehensible it is to non-Jews. If you're Jewish, and you miss a day of work, and your non-Jewish employer asks you why, all you have to do is say, "I was observing the Jewish holiday of Y'shem V'atoah." Your employer will immediately apologize for questioning you, even though there is no such holiday as Y'shem V'atoah. At least we don't think there is. We're not 100 percent sure. And we're an encyclopedia.

NOTE: We are not condoning the practice of making up Jewish holidays to get out of work. That would be wrong, and you should not do it more than three or four times a year.

Speaking of years: The Jewish calendar starts with Creation, which occurred on the Gregorian calendar date of October 7, 3761 B.C., according to the teachings of Rabbi Yose ben Halafta, who was a teenager at the time. So if you want to know what year it is according to the Jewish calendar, you simply add 3760 to the current Gregorian year if it's before Rosh Hashanah, or 3761 if it's after Rosh Hashanah. In other words, google it.

SHABBAT

What a hectic week the Lord had when He created everything!
According to Genesis 1, this was the Supreme Being's to-do list:

DAY 1—DAY AND NIGHT
DAY 2—SKY AND SEA
DAY 3—LAND AND VEGETATION
DAY 4—STARS, SUN, AND MOON
DAY 5—SEA CREATURES, FISH, AND BIRDS
DAY 6—ANIMALS AND MANKIND

Then is it any wonder that he rested on the seventh day—walking around heaven in his pajamas and eating leftovers from what he made on days 3, 5, and 6?

This day of rest is called "Shabbat," a word that comes from the Hebrew root *shin-beit-tav,* which means "Hey, everybody, Shabbat is so darn important that it has a three-word root from which it is derived."

And so important is this day that it is considered to be so much holier than even Yom Kippur—the highest of the High Holidays—that it's the only ritual observance mentioned in the Ten Commandments. "Remember the Sabbath Day and keep it holy" is the third commandment, right after "Thou shalt not take the name of the Lord in vain" and just before "Honor thy mother and thy father," so one can only imagine what kind of hot water they're in if they say, "G-d damn you, Mom, those shoes make you look like a two-bit hooker" on a Saturday.

Shabbat is considered sacred for two reasons. The first is to remember that if the Lord's work can be set aside for a day of rest, how can we believe that our work is too important not to do the same? For example, and with all due respect to plumbers, if the Lord kicked back after creating the entire universe, couldn't an oversized man whose butt crack is now the reigning logo of his profession wait until Sunday to drain that pan under a refrigerator?

The second reason is that in Egypt the slaves did not have a day of rest, so Shabbat is, in present-day ideology, a day celebrating freedom from our bosses, creditors, and all other concerns that hound us during the week. Once the candles are lit and the arms have been waved in a uniting, world-gathering motion to welcome the onset of Shabbat, all mundane worries are put on hold until sundown the following day. The one hitch in this scenario, which has confounded the rabbis for centuries, is what happens if someone makes their living as an arm-waving candle lighter, so he or she is, in effect, working on the Sabbath? And since there are fifty-two Shabbats a year and the average person lives to be seventy-eight years old, would that sinner be going to hell, if Jews indeed believed in such a place?

Exactly what specific work is prohibited on the Sabbath is the source of some confusion, because what was considered to be work in biblical times, such as plowing, reaping, threshing, shearing wool, curing hide, etc., is not exactly what the present-day Sabbath observer does to begin with. So an observant Jew's refraining from an activity like binding sheaves is no major (as the kids say) to-do.

Over time, as new inventions have appeared, rabbis have been asked to render decisions on their usage during Shabbat. Actions taken to complete a circuit, such as turning on an electric light switch, starting the engine of a car, or even carrying money (because it is used to complete transactions) fall into a sacred category known as לא שבת (Shabbat no-nos).

Further clarity concerning what can and can't be done on the Sabbath has been provided by an updated definition of *melachah,* a term that refers to labor that gives one control over the environment, such as the control G-d exhibited with creation. That's why turning on a lamp to brighten a dark room or renting a small plane and seeding the clouds to make it rain are restricted activities. Though exactly why Orthodox Jews must pre-tear toilet paper before the onset of Shabbat is still a mystery, as logic dictates that the rending of two-ply requires a lot less energy than its actual use.

SHABBOS GOY

Even so, Jews have found loopholes in the concept of *melachah* to circumvent certain Shabbat restrictions by employing a non-Jew called a "Shabbos goy" to perform duties prohibited during the Sabbath. That, or beginning the *melachah* actions before the onset of Shabbat and allowing them to continue throughout. So, for instance, if you turn on a light before sundown on Friday, you can leave it on during the entire Sabbath. The same applies to the women of the house turning a flame on a stove before sundown on Friday so the Sabbath meal can be cooked the following day or the health nut who starts doing jumping jacks in the back of a moving EMS transport before sundown on Friday so he can be rushed to the hospital by a Gentile driver if he has a heart attack on the Sabbath.

We would write more on this holy topic, but it's now late on a Friday afternoon and we have to start tearing toilet paper to use during the Sabbath lest we change the environment in ways we don't wish to get into.

DISCUSSION QUESTIONS FOR "SHABBAT"

- Does it seem weird to you guys that Hashem made Day and Night several days before the Sun, Stars, and Moon?
- It is yours to question, smart guy?
- How many cosmos have YOU created?
- Could there be a hit Hollywood movie called *Shabbos Goy*? Hold on, just hear us out: It's a thriller that takes place in a Hasidic community—let's say it's the Satmars in Williamsburg, Brooklyn. Boom, so okay, there's a heist on Shabbat—somebody breaks into the Grand Rebbe's house and steals thirty years' worth of financial shit—bank records and all kinds of very valuable and sensitive information—all of which is kept in a filing cabinet because these dudes do not use computers. The thief puts on his infrared glasses or whatever and just walks in, turns out all the lights—which nobody dares turn back on—he's in and out, jumps in a car. The Satmars can only run after him, because driving is work—so the thief escapes. The only guy who can give chase and recover the stolen goods before all hell breaks loose is . . . THE SHABBOS GOY. Played by Jason Statham, we're thinking. Tell me you couldn't sell that in a room.

ROSH HASHANAH

Rosh Hashanah is the Jewish New Year. It is celebrated on the first day of Tishrei, which is the seventh month of the year, but it is when the year number changes. Do not confuse Rosh Hashanah with the beginning of the religious year, on the first of Nisan, or with Tu B'Shvat, which marks the beginning of the new year for trees. Nor with the fiscal new year, on which cattle were taxed in ancient times, which commences on the first of Elul.

Naturally, all this raises some questions, such as: How do trees celebrate the new year? And how can cows afford accountants? For answers to these questions, you can consult Appendix F.* For now, an easy way to determine whether it is Rosh Hashanah is to go to

---

* Though not in this book.

Williamsburg, Brooklyn, and see whether anyone is swinging a live rooster over their head in circles. If so, you are witnessing the ancient ritual of *kapparah* ("poultry abuse").

Rosh Hashanah and Yom Kippur, which comes ten days later, are collectively known as the High Holidays. Unlike the rest of the Jewish holidays, they commemorate neither a time we narrowly escaped annihilation nor a time we harvested some grain. Instead, these holidays ask us to look inward and examine our relationship with the Capo di Tutti Capi.

Unlike the goyish new year, Rosh Hashanah is no time to stand in the middle of Times Square freezing your entire ass off alongside ten thousand other drunken morons who are not from New York City. Indeed, Rosh Hashanah is also called the Day of Remembrance and the Day of Judgment, which ought to offer a great big hint about how much fun this is gonna be even before we get to:

THE BOOK OF DEATH

According to the Talmud, on Rosh Hashanah G-d spreads out three books on His desk—which, trust us, He did not purchase at Ikea, if you know what we mean. These books are the Book of Death, the Book of Life, and the Book Which Oddly Has No Name Even Though It Is the Central Book in This Talmudic Metaphor. One book is for the names of the wicked, one is for the names of the righteous, and one is for the names of those who are in between. These in-betweeners have until Yom Kippur to pray, repent, perform acts of charity, and do abhorrent centrifugal violence unto chickens, in the hopes of getting moved to a better book.

Of course, this "judgment" is just a metaphor* intended to get us to reflect on the year that just passed and ask ourselves difficult questions like:

---

* Unless it's not.

- Were there times you were kind of a dick?
- Were there people you hurt this year, either unintentionally or for money?
- Could you have negotiated for more money?
- Are you fulfilling the dreams and promises you set for yourself?
- What about your mother's dream of having some grandchildren before she's dead? Have you fulfilled that?
- Seriously, though—you know you were kind of a dick, right?

HOW TO CELEBRATE

The High Holidays are the only time of the entire year that many Jews set foot in a synagogue, assuaging their guilt at not attending more frequently by paying more for tickets than their grandparents paid for a college education.

These Jews may thus get the impression that everybody at their ("their") synagogue is very well dressed. But this is false; most of these people are actually quite schlubby. Rosh Hashanah is just a time for them to get dressed up. It is also a time, the Torah tells us, to blow the ram's horn known as the shofar one hundred times, in various ways, throughout the Rosh Hashanah services.

For many Jews, the plaintive sounds of the shofar carry deep spiritual significance. It is said to be the sound the Israelites heard at Mount Sinai, and it is said that G-d will blow the shofar again to signal the coming of the Messiah. To some it is a call to wake up, either spiritually or from the light slumber than has befallen us after hours in an increasingly fart-filled synagogue. Even if the blast of the shofar merely sounds to you like the noise a large dinosaur might make while being pleasured, remember that it has been a constant throughout our thousands of years as a ram-eating people.

A two-day holiday, Rosh Hashanah begins with a lighting of candles at sundown. But there are surprisingly few unique rituals involved in the holiday aside from the candle lighting and the blowing of the shofar. Mostly, you pray and pray some more. Maybe you pray for an end to the prayers. Perhaps you make a couple of terrible jokes about single-prayer coverage.

There is also the custom of *tashlikh*, in which we visit a body of free-flowing water and empty our pockets and cuffs of lint and crumbs to symbolize the kind of blatant disregard for both our waterways and our personal hygiene that we have resolved to improve upon in the coming year.

THE MENU

It is customary to eat sweet foods, especially apples dipped in honey, and toast to a "sweet year." Round challah with raisins is also customary, as roundness symbolizes the cycle of life. Hamburgers covered in sugar are both sweet and round, as are six-month-old hamantaschen bitten into circular shapes.

Some people also like to add dishes to the meal based on puns. For example, if you invite a single friend to the meal you might offer dates with the wish, "May you enjoy many sweet dates this year." Or if you invite Mel Gibson to Rosh Hashanah, you might hand him a plate of tripe and remark, "Look, you're not the only sack of shit here."

Another customary dish is tzimmes, a casserole of carrots, sweet potatoes, and prunes that is almost as appetizing as it sounds. And of course, no Jewish New Year would be complete without a massive helping of kugel, a sweet noodle pudding that will lie in your gut like a rock until your final Rosh Hashanah.

In addition to these special treats, you may also want to serve some food.

ROSH HASHITHEAD

While holidays are days generally fixed by law or custom to commemorate some event or in honor of some person, Rosh Hashithead is a joyous holiday that will not find a place on the Jewish calendar until Mel Gibson dies.

Exactly when the celebration of the demise of this anti-Semite will commence is anyone's guess, as longevity appears to be a dominant trait in the Gibson family. As of this writing, Gibson's Holocaust-denying father, Hutton, is one hundred years old and appears to still be going strong, following a daily workout regimen that includes eradicating the letters "J," "E," and "W" from the New Testament and sustaining himself on a diet where he only eats small pieces of Adolf Hitler. But whenever Mel does pass away, this holiday will be celebrated annually, marked by kosher delicatessens being closed and parades in front of Charlie Sheen's house.

YOM KIPPUR

This is the Big One. The biggest Jewish holiday of the year. How big? Well, let's just say that if the other Jewish holidays are NBA players, Yom Kippur is LeBron James. If they are planets, Yom Kippur is Jupiter. If they are the Trump administration, Yom Kippur is anyone else's administration.

This is the Day of Atonement, the most solemn day when we ask G-d to forgive us for all the horrible things we did the preceding year—everything from major sins like cheating on your spouse to lesser infractions like cutting off an ambulance on its way to the hospital. And what if you feel that Yom Kippur is irrelevant for you because you did absolutely nothing wrong, therefore you have nothing to repent for? Well, in that case, please feel free to add our names to the long list of people who'd prefer not to be in the company of anyone who thinks they've never made a mistake.

ORIGIN OF YOM KIPPUR

How did this Day of Atonement come about? Historically, it harkens back to when the Hebrew slaves came out of Egypt and committed a terrible crime in the desert when they made a golden calf and worshipped it. And then Moses, who had a BFF relationship with the Almighty, had to plead with Him for forty days and forty nights on behalf of the slaves until he could gain His forgiveness. The date that G-d relented and allowed His mercy to override the transgression was on the tenth of Tishrei, so that became the Day of Atonement for future generations, although Moses was confused by this entire episode.

"Why are you mad at me?" he asked G-d. "I was up on Mount Sinai receiving your commandments when they built that golden calf. I had nothing to do with it."

And the Lord mimicked Moses. "I had nothing to do with it. I had nothing to do with it. Jesus, you're annoying."

"Jesus?"

"Oh, right. Just keep walking."

OBSERVING YOM KIPPUR

While most Jewish holidays are distinguished by what you can do, it is much easier to describe Yom Kippur by what you can't do. Here's a partial list:

Work
Play
Bathe

Anoint oneself with perfume or moisturizers

Have sex. (Although, seriously, who would want to have sex with anyone who hasn't bathed or dabbed themselves with perfume to disguise the accompanying stench?)

All of the no-nos of Shabbat. (In fact, Yom Kippur is often referred to as "The Shabbat of All Shabbats," which is similar to that popular adage that Thanksgiving is the "Shabbat of All Thursdays.")

In a nutshell, you can't do anything—which includes eating the nut that was in that nutshell because you aren't supposed to eat or drink anything for twenty-four hours.

FASTING

Why do we fast? Why do Jews not eat from sundown the night before (*erev* Yom Kippur) to sundown the next night (*after* Kippur)?

The rabbis claim that because eating gives you pleasure, the denial of this satisfaction gives you little choice but to focus on your prayers and spiritual energies of the day—as opposed to the loud stomach rumblings of all the hungry penitents seated around you, which only serves to intensify the headache you already have from not eating.

Just as there are conditions that make a young man or woman exempt from conscription into the armed services, a Jewish person is excused from fasting if he or she:

Is under the age of thirteen

Is very ill

Is very pregnant

Is recovering from a serious operation

Converts to another religion before Yom Kippur kicks in and then rejoins the tribe after sundown the next day

THINGS YOU CAN DO WHILE WAITING FOR SUNSET

Given the limitations on allowable activity, other than sitting in a synagogue and praying that the hands on your wristwatch move at breakneck speed so you can eat again, here is a list of suggestions of things you can do to pass the time:

Sit across from a friend or family member and stare at each other for the next twenty-four hours.

Buy a can of paint before sundown on *erev* Yom Kippur, apply it to one of the walls in your house, and watch the paint dry for the next twenty-four hours.

Find a hibernating bear, lie down next to him, and mimic everything he does for the next twenty-four hours.

Find someone who makes that joke about being allowed to eat McDonald's on Yom Kippur because it's "fast food" and beat the shit out of him.

ONE SECOND AFTER THE SUN SETS

Stuff your face like you're going to the electric chair and resume making the same mistakes you just asked to be forgiven for until next Yom Kippur, when you ask for forgiveness once again.

BOOK OF LIFE

On Rosh Hashanah G-d opens the Book of Life and during the next ten days (also known as Days of Awe) He determines the fate of all Jews before He seals the book on Yom Kippur. After Yom Kippur He decides who shall live and who shall die. Who shall be rich, and who shall be poor. Who shall be thin, and who shall need the police to use the Jaws of Life to extricate them from their bathtub.

You may be wondering, does G-d have an actual book or is this an allegory? Perhaps this story will shed some light on this question. The Talmud tells of two dead rabbis who were walking down a street in heaven when they spotted G-d struggling to carry the very large, very thick Book of Life.

"Shouldn't he have someone carrying that for him?" asked the first dead rabbi.

"What do you care? We're not in it," said the second dead rabbi.

"Yeah, I hope he throws his back out," replied the first dead rabbi.

FORGIVENESS

We are all human beings and we all make mistakes. So we are encouraged to forgive each other before we can expect G-d to forgive us. To accomplish this, the rabbis tell us to take a look at the bigger picture when judging others. For example, if a child is a whiny, obnoxious turd, it may be very easy for you to get angry with him. But if you take the time to examine his complete set of circumstances and discover that he comes from a broken home, you are more apt to forgive his behavior even if you still choose to avoid him like the plague because, really, who needs an obnoxious, whiny turd in their lives?

The rabbis describe a three-step approach to forgiveness. The first is to have a conscious intent to forgive. The second is to let go of the past—to no longer hold on to the resentment of having once been wronged. The last is atonement, which transforms prior ill feelings into blessings.

And like so many ancient Jewish practices, their benefits are also supported by the modern medical community, as psychologists agree that forgiveness is an empowering approach that ultimately leads to a state of cognitive consonance. Endocrinologists concur by asserting that secretions associated with the act of atonement lead to a state of placidity. The list goes on, with only one exception among physicians, but the authors of this book are far too classy to make any cheap jokes about how proctologists say they see no reason to make peace with any pains in the ass, so let's move on.

THE MIRACLE OF JONAH

The Book of Jonah tells of the Hebrew prophet named Jonah, son of Amittai, great-nephew of Betty White, who was asked by G-d to go warn the hedonistic residents of Nineveh to repent or they would face the Lord's divine wrath in forty days. But Jonah wanted nothing to do with the Ninevites, who were not only major enemies of the Jews but whose name he had trouble pronouncing.

So, instead, he tried to run away from G-d by heading in the opposite direction of Nineveh and boarded a ship bound for Tarsish—a town that wasn't exactly Tars but was Tars-ish. G-d, less than pleased at Jonah's disobedience, sent a great storm upon the ship, and the men, figuring that Jonah was to blame, threw him overboard. The sailors may have been on to something, because the moment Jonah hit the water, the storm stopped and the raging sea turned calm. "We should've done this earlier," said the ship's captain. "That rain drenched my sheepskin slicker and now I'm shaking, swaying, and spinning the way Abraham's wife Sarah did after she gave birth to Isaac at the age of ninety."

G-d, on the other hand, took pity on the now drowning Jonah and sent a whale to swallow him. That's right, a whale. G-d did not save Jonah by sending him a lifeboat, or swimmies, or causing a strong wind to lift him up and deposit him gently onto a nearby beach. No, instead the Lord saw fit to have Jonah spend three days inside the belly of a sheltering whale, where he prayed for forgiveness, read magazines, practiced his boxing on the whale's uvula, and thanked the Lord for not having him swallowed by a mackerel, which would've offered more cramped quarters.

Just how G-d discharged Jonah from the whale has been a matter of debate among rabbinical scholars for centuries, with one school claiming that the nauseous whale vomited Jonah onto the shores of Nineveh and another saying that the flatulent whale farted Jonah onto the shores of Nineveh. Either way, Jonah warned the Ninevites about G-d's wrath and the Ninevites changed their ways and G-d spared them.

This story, read every year during the afternoon service on Yom Kippur to illustrate G-d's willingness to forgive those who repent, unfortunately had an unhappy ending for Jonah, who shortly afterward went swimming and was swallowed up again, this time by a flu-stricken whale who sneezed and sent Jonah shooting out of his blowhole back onto the shores of Nineveh, where he got beaten to a pulp by the Ninevites, who had been having a lot more fun before Jonah opened his big mouth.

SUKKOTH

The festival of Sukkoth begins on the fifth day after Yom Kippur, which is quite a contrast—going from the solemnity of a holiday where you can't eat or drink for twenty-four hours to one where you stuff your face with everything you can get your hands on. In fact, Sukkoth is so unreservedly joyful that it is commonly referred to in Jewish prayer and literature as זְמַן שִׂמְחָתֵנוּ, which means "one of the few holidays when we aren't complaining about anything."

Sukkoth has a dual significance. Historically, it commemorates the forty years that the children of Israel spent wandering in the desert living in temporary shelters, while agriculturally, Sukkoth is the festival of the harvest—an interesting combo platter given that one has to wonder exactly how many fruits and vegetables could possibly have been harvested while roaming the desert for four decades that it would warrant a holiday.

So let's concentrate on those shelters, shall we? The word "Sukkah" means "booth" (as in Lincoln's assassin John Wilkes Sukkah) and refers to those temporary dwellings that we are commanded to live in during this holiday in memory of the period of wandering. No matter where you live, whether it be a hovel or mansion, you are required to move into a three-sided thatched hut for a full week, with the open side facing west so it will serve as a welcoming entrance to all visitors traveling east. As for those travelers traveling west, well, since you don't have an opening to enter through, you have two choices: either walk around the *sukkah* and enter via the open side, or retrace your steps until you circumvent the entire globe and are now approaching the east from the west. The rabbis tell us that the choice between these two options depends on just how much time our bosses will allow us to take off from work.

It is customary to decorate the *sukkah* (singular form of *sukkoth*, which is the plural form, oddly enough, of "Sucrets") with hanging dried squash and corn, as these vegetables are readily available at that time for Thanksgiving—a festive American holiday that resembles Sukkoth except for the fact that no one, even the most religious Jews, hangs dried turkeys from the roof of their *sukkah*.

Another ritual during Sukkoth involves what are known as the Four Species, which are four plants that are used to rejoice before the Lord. The plants are: an etrog (citrus fruit similar to a lemon), a palm branch (called a *lulav* in Hebrew), two willow branches, and three myrtle branches. After they are bound together, they are held by the rabbi during a procession around the bimah (the raised platform in the synagogue upon which Torah portions are read) each day of Sukkoth. On the seventh day of the holiday, seven circuits are made around the bimah before the rabbi gets dizzy, stumbles down the stairs, and collapses to serve as a reminder that Sukkoth is now over and the *sukkah* should be taken down.

CHANUKAH

Chanukah—also spelled Chanuka, Chanukkah, Chihuahua, Chardonnay, Hanukah, Hannukah, Hannnnnukah, Hannah, Hanukkah, Hanuka, Honeydew, Haneka, Hanika, and Khanukkah—is perhaps the most celebrated and best-known Jewish holiday, probably because it involves giving gifts and eating fried food rather than contemplating sin or waving citrus at strangers.

But there is another reason for Chanukah's popularity. It happens to fall in December, which is when the four-month Christmas shopping season culminates with a festive goyish day on which an ancient married couple's failure to have sexual intercourse is celebrated by the wearing of hideous sweaters, the opening of gifts said to be built by elves from the far north and delivered by an obese man who rides a sleigh pulled by reindeer, and the eating of ham beneath a recently murdered pine tree atop which a replica of an angel has been impaled.

Christmas is not a Jewish holiday, though it does celebrate the birth of a Jewish dude and all the best songs about it were written by Jewish dudes, and also Jews keep our national economy afloat on that day through our support of the Chinese restaurant and film industries. But the role Christmas has played in elevating Chanukah from a relatively obscure holiday to a major one cannot be denied, because once Jewish children realized how much swag their Christian friends were getting on December 25, they clamored to learn more about the victory of Jewish freedom fighters over the Syrian-Greek forces in the second century B.C.E.

THE STORY OF CHANUKAH

During the reign of Alexander the Great, everybody was free to practice whatever religion they wanted. This was what made Alexander so Great: he'd sweep in, conquer the crap out of a country, and then just be like, "As you were, country." Maybe you had to pay some taxes or whatever, but for the most part things were pretty chill. Then Alexander died, and the empire split into empirelets, many of them ruled by total bozos.

One of these bozos was Antiochus ("Against Ochus"), who promptly outlawed—on pain of death—kosher food, circumcision, Shabbat services, and kvetching. This drove a wedge into the Jewish community: On one side were the "Hellenists," assimilated Jews who were into Greek art and philosophy and perfectly char-grilled octopus with fresh oregano and potatoes and just the right amount of drizzled olive oil. On the other side were the more, how shall we put it . . . psychotically enthusiastic worshippers of Hashem. Their leader was Mattathias, a priestly descendant of Moses's brother Aaron.

One day, Mattathias came across a Hellenist making a sacrifice to the Greek gods. So Mattathias killed him, because it says right in the Ten Commandments that you're not allowed to worship other gods, shortly before it says you're not allowed to kill.

Then, in the great tradition of revolutionaries fleeing into the mountains with their five sons, Mattathias fled into the mountains with his five sons. Other bloodthirsty religious types soon joined him, and they formed an army to fight both Antiochus's forces and the Hellenist Jews. When Mattathias died, his son Judah took over, and he was such a badass that people started calling him Judah Maccabee, or "Judah Hammer," which inspired his followers to start calling themselves "Maccabees" and for Judah to embark upon a career in professional wrestling once the bloody three-year war concluded.

THE MIRACLE OF THE OIL

Finally, Judah and the Maccabees (with the help of Martha Reeves and the Vandellas) came down from the mountains, drove out the Syrian-Greek army, retook Jerusalem, and started restoring the Second Temple. They commemorated this occasion with an eight-day celebration, which we'll get to in a minute. Also, we apologize for the misleading bold-print heading of this section, which as it turns out has nothing to do with oil.

HISTORY IS WEIRD SOMETIMES

Maybe you're saying to yourself, "Why isn't the focus of Chanukah this gnarly three-year guerrilla war led by a ruggedly handsome warrior with a cool nickname? That seems more epic by far than the fact that afterward they cleaned up the temple and the 164 B.C.E. equivalent of a lightbulb exceeded its warranty." It's a great question, which is why we are pretending you asked it. The answer is that by the time the Talmud was written, not everybody was such a huge Maccabee fanboy. For one thing, the Maccabees—like many revolutionary-armies-turned-governments—were oppressive and brutal once they gained power. Also, their descendants got in bed with the Roman Empire (it was a large bed), which eventually led to getting conquered by Rome, which any student of history will tell you totally sucked. Certainly, no one could have predicted any of this from the beginning of the story, when Mattathias murders that dude in cold blood merely for obeying a law the poor schmuck would have been killed for disobeying.

THE MIRACLE OF THE OIL

According to Legend,* the Maccabees could only find one vessel of olive oil in the temple, enough to keep the Eternal Flame burning for a single night. It would take eight days to get more oil—which seems like a very long time, until you consider that the oil had to be both consecrated by a high priest and certified organic—but G-d performed a miracle and made the oil last for eight nights.

CHANUKAH RITUALS AND CUSTOMS

THE MENORAH

The thing you call a menorah is actually called a *chanukiah*. It has nine candleholders, and your only real Chanukah duty, aside from buying your children enough presents that they do not defect to Christianity, is to light them, using the central candle (the *shammash*) to light the others (the *candles*)—one on the first night, two on the second night, and so on. You should light them from right to left, and you shouldn't use their light to do your taxes by or start forest fires with, because these candles are just for looking and remembering a time when olive oil was not readily available at Whole Foods.

Some families take turns lighting the candles, with each child

---

* Ezekiel Greenblatt Legend, 35–1 B.C.E.

scheming on how to light more candles than his or her siblings over the course of the festival, but only a few of them being good enough at math to actually figure it out. In other households, everyone holds the *shammash* together, trading bickering for first-degree burns.

EATING FRIED FOODS BECAUSE: OIL

The most common oily Chanukah treats are potato latkes, served with applesauce and sour cream, and Israeli *sufganiot* (jelly doughnuts). You can find recipes for both in the back of this book, assuming that we remember to write them.

But there is no reason to stop there! Another fun Chanukah ritual is to set up a deep fryer and just go nuts. There is nothing you can't improve by frying it in hot oil, including this book.

SPINNING THE DREIDEL

The dreidel is a four-sided top imprinted with the Hebrew letters *nun, gimel, hay,* and *shin,* the initials of which stand for the phrase *Nes gadol hayah sham* ("I'm taking all you suckers' money!").

Each player starts with a pile of candies, nuts, Bitcoins, prerolled joints, dead squirrels, etc. Before each turn, everyone antes up. Then someone spins the dreidel.

If it lands on *nun,* nothing happens—unless you are a nun, in which case you lose a turn. Also, you are no longer a nun.

If it lands on *gimel,* you win the pot. It is considered bad manners to get up and leave at this point.

If it lands on *hay,* each player is awarded a bale of hay from the communal hay stash.

If it lands on *shin,* each player kicks the player to their left in the shin.

The origins of this game are mysterious, but one theory is that it started at a time (pick one) when Jews were forbidden to study Torah. To avoid being caught, they'd pull out their dreidels and pretend to be gambling. Let's recap that: *the Jews would pretend to gamble so they could study.* If that doesn't perfectly sum up the beauty and lameness of Judaism, we don't know what does.

DISCUSSION QUESTIONS FOR "CHANUKAH"

- Some Jewish families buy a "Chanukah bush" and claim that the presents under it are from a Santa Claus–like figure named "Chanukah Harry." What do you think stops these families from also taking communion?
- The Chanukah story is a good example of how a story can evolve over time, to reflect changing political realities. In your opinion, how could this be phrased as a thought-provoking question?
- Let's say that the hottest Transformer on the late-1980s holiday market is a totally badass Autobot plane named Jetfire, and let's also say that both your kids are consumed by a burning passion to own this toy, even though it will inevitably break within weeks, because unlike the

indestructible titanium of the Japanese versions of these toys that will go on to be valuable collectors' items and prized family heirlooms, the plastic American knockoffs begin melting within minutes of being placed on a radiator, and also they can only halfway transform once they get a little bit of sand in them. If you were to buy Jetfire for one of your kids and a calculator for the other, do you think it would scar the kid who received the calculator so badly that he ended up being a comedy writer?

TU B'SHVAT

Tu B'Shvat is one of those Jewish holidays that the majority of American Jews have never heard of. And of those American Jews who have heard of it, the majority don't know what the holiday is for. And for those American Jews who do know what the holiday is for, the majority feel that it falls squarely into the category of "who gives a shit?"

To begin with, Tu B'Shvat is the fifteenth day of the month of Shevat. "Tu" is a combination of the letters *tet* and *vav*, which have the numerical values of 9 and 6, which add up to 15—hence, the name Tu B'Shvat means the fifteenth of Shevat, so the holiday is named for the date it falls on with no hint whatsoever of what it signifies. Think about it. Yom Kippur is the Day of Atonement. Rosh Hashanah means head of the year. Passover implies the angel

of death that passed over Jewish homes the night before the Hebrew slaves left Egypt. The holiday names all have hints as to why
they exist. But the fifteenth of Shevat? Tantamount to our having a
holiday called "August 12" for no reason other than the fact that it
falls on August 12. Again, who gives a shit?

But let's dig deeper, shall we? According to the rabbis, Tu B'Shvat,
despite its ill-conceived name, is actually the celebration of Israel's
planting season—similar to our Arbor Day. Okay, that's a step in
the right direction. But when does the fifteenth day of Shevat fall
on our calendar? Anywhere from late January to early February.
The dead of winter. The time of year when you can see your breath
and have to start warming up your car a week before you have to use
it. Planting? Seriously? Ever try to plunge a shovel into the frozen
earth on Super Bowl Sunday? Or have to rent a plow to move high
drifts of wet snow before getting down on your knees to plant an
azalea bush on Groundhog Day—a day whose name lets you know
what it's for, by the way?

As for you Jewish Floridians, Jewish Californians, Jewish Ari-
zonans, etc., whose weather allows for planting in late January and
early February, fine. Plant your asses off to your heart's delight. But
good luck with your boss when you tell him you can't come to work
that day because you're observing Tu B'Shvat. Or after telling your
college professor that you can't take your history midterm because
it's the beginning of the planting season in Israel. We recommend
that you brace yourself in preparation for the response of "You're
fired!" Or "You failed!" Or, more likely, "Who gives a shit?"

PURIM

The story of Purim begins in Ancient Persia (now known as Persia), during the reign of King Ahasuerus (often written as Akhashveyrosh, and sometimes translated as Xerxes), a legendarily fun guy who had the political acumen of a medium-rare hamster. All Ahasuerus cared about was making up outlandish names for himself and throwing lavish parties.

At one such party—said to have lasted 180 days, which was absolute murder on the caterers—he got super drunk and demanded that his queen, Vashti, dance naked before the court. Vashti refused, and before she could even file a lawsuit alleging that Ahasuerus had created an unsafe workplace environment, Ahasuerus had her exiled. Vashti was like, "Is that supposed to be a *punishment*?" and promptly left the Hebrew Bible, never to return.

This left the king in need of a queen. After a futile and depressing few months on Tinder, Ahasuerus decided to induct a few dozen virgins into his personal harem and audition one per night until one of them met his criteria for queendom, which probably did not involve the ability to perform complex acts of trigonometry.

It so happened that a Jewish fellow by the name of Mordecai worked in the palace. His cousin Esther, whom he had adopted after her parents died from eating poorly spiced lamb kebabs, was among the women called to appear before the king. Mordecai advised her not to reveal that she was Jewish. Esther pointed out that her name was Esther, which seemed like kind of a dead giveaway, but Mordecai assured her that the king was not the sharpest cudgel in the cudgel storage facility, so Esther was like, okay, whatever.

As one might expect in a story from the Book of Esther, Esther became the new queen. And as the weeks went by, she was very careful not to reveal herself, going so far as to pay retail on three distinct occasions. Also, in one of the most remarkable feats of restraint in Jewish history, *every single Jew in the kingdom refrained from pointing out that the queen was Jewish, no matter how much* nachas *it gave them.*

Then one day, Mordecai learned of a plot by two eunuchs to assassinate the king. He told Esther, who told Ahasuerus, who had the eunuchs hung—which is ironic, if you think about it. All this was dutifully written down in the official court chronicle, which nobody ever actually got around to reading—it was the Ancient Persian equivalent of one of Tom Wolfe's later novels—and life was uneventful until the day Ahasuerus sobered up long enough to appoint a dude named Haman as prime minister.

Haman was such a schmuck that he demanded everybody bow down to him. Like, literally bow down. Not that it is possible to bow up. Anyhoo, Mordecai refused, because Jews only bow to G-d, and apparently his advice to Esther about laying low, religion-wise, before a king who couldn't possibly have cared less did not extend to exercising an ounce of discretion himself when dealing with an unstable megalomaniacal douchecanoe. And sure enough, Haman decided to punish Mordecai's disobedience by—wait for it—killing every last Jew in the kingdom.

Ahasuerus was like, "Could be fun," and issued a decree that on the thirteenth of Adar, anybody and everybody was allowed to kill Jews with impunity and claim their property. At this point, Mordecai changed his tune and told Esther she had to approach the king, come clean, and talk some sense into him. Esther was reluctant, because Ancient Persia had a law—originally established to discourage Jehovah's Witnesses—that anybody who appeared before the king without an invitation faced instant death.

But luckily, Ahasuerus was pretty chill about it, and he invited Esther to make a request of him. This threw Esther for a loop. What could she possibly ask for? Thinking quickly, she asked the king . . . to have dinner with her, and bring Haman.

Ahasuerus agreed. At the banquet, Esther mustered all her courage and . . . asked them both to have dinner with her again the following night. Who knows how long she would have kept this up. But luckily, that night the king couldn't sleep, and he figured that having the court chronicles read to him might do the trick. Thus did Ahasuerus learn that some schlemiel named Mordecai had foiled the assassination plot—and also that he'd never been rewarded for it. So the king called Haman and asked him what ought to be done for a man whom the king wishes to honor.

Haman, who always thought everything was about him, told Ahasuerus that the thing to do was dress the guy up in the finest royal robes, and put him on a horse, and then put the horse on an elephant, and then put the elephant on top of a mountain of cocaine, and have an attendant lead them all through the streets shouting, "This is how the king treats his homies, scumbags!"

Ahasuerus was like, "Cool, I'm doing that for Mordecai tomorrow, and you can be the shouty guy." Haman was super pissed but he had to do it. What does this have to do with anything? Nothing, really. But it does explain what kind of mood Haman was in when he showed up for dinner the following night, at which point Esther finally revealed that she was Jewish, and so was her cousin Mordecai, and thus Haman's plan would result in both their deaths, to say nothing of what it would do to the Ancient Persian gefilte fish industry.

It was a tense moment. They both watched Ahasuerus carefully as he worked his way methodically through seven more courses and a bottle and a half of schnapps. Finally, he shrugged and decided to hang Haman on the very gallows Haman had built for Mordecai. Obviously, there were already gallows around, because Ahasuerus had hung the eunuchs there, but apparently Haman had commissioned an entirely new set of gallows, possibly as part of a stimulus initiative.

So Haman was finished, but there was still the matter of the decree allowing the festive slaughter of the Jews. In a move that really puts our own dysfunctional government in perspective, the king refused to just reverse it, possibly for fear of looking like he was in the pocket of a certain Globalist Cabal, if you know what we mean. So instead, he issued a second decree that the Jews were allowed to fight back. And indeed, when the thirteenth of Adar rolled around, the Jews were ready. They kicked the living crapola out of their enemies, killing seventy-five thousand of them in a massive, epic battle that is mostly a distant afterthought to this story of palace intrigue and meddlesome cousins, and is almost never discussed.

WHO IS NOT IN THE BOOK OF ESTHER: A PARTIAL LIST

You may have noticed that there's Somebody missing from the Book of Esther. Indeed, it is the only book of the Hebrew Bible in which the Big Fella does not appear. Some rabbis teach that this is because He is always present—even when He is not named, even when He cannot be felt, even when things are at their worst. Other rabbis contend that this is exactly the kind of claptrap you'd expect from *those* rabbis, and that Adonai our G-d is not present because the Book of Esther is like that episode of *Atlanta* where Earn, Paper Boi, and Darius aren't even in it, and it's just Vanessa and her friend going on that weird double date with those guys. Still other rabbis have not seen *Atlanta,* even though it's probably the best show on TV right now.

CELEBRATING PURIM

READING THE BOOK OF ESTHER

The Book of Esther is written on a single scroll, which is called a megillah. On Purim, the whole story is read aloud, which is the origin of the popular expression "Oy vey."

It is traditional, whenever Haman's name is read, to drown it out by booing, hissing, twirling noisemakers, smashing giant crystal punch bowls with mallets, or revving the engines of Harley-Davidson motorcycles. Some people take the ritual even further, writing Haman's name on their shoes and then vomiting on them, which leads us to . . .

PUBLIC DRUNKENNESS

The majority of Jews—and *all* of the world's alcoholics, regardless of religion—believe in getting hammered on Purim, and not in the Maccabee sense of the word. Indeed, there is a rabbinical commandment to "drink until you don't know the difference between *Arur Haman* ('Cursed is Haman') and *Barukh Mordecai* ('Blessed is Mordecai')." For Reform Jews, this may not require any alcohol at all.

OTHER CUSTOMS

If invited to a Purim party, it is important to ask whether you should wear a costume (this is a good practice for all parties), because Purim is basically the Jewish Halloween, a day on which we dress up, snarf down mammoth amounts of sweets, and TP the crap out of Johnny Hotchkiss's house.

Popular Purim costumes include Haman, Esther, Esther Williams, and Esther Rolle. There is no "wrong" costume to wear to a Purim party, though you should probably think twice before showing up naked save for an adult-sized diaper.

At a Purim party, you might also witness—or, after enough brandy, participate in—a *purimspiel,* a play loosely based on the Book of Esther. The vast majority of Jewish actors—including Tony Curtis (born Bernard Schwartz), Natalie Portman, and Lupita Nyong'o (born Aviva Himmelfarb)—were discovered at *purimspiels.*

Finally, plan to eat plenty of hamantaschen ("Haman's pocket"), a delicious three-cornered cookie. If it strikes you as odd, or even distasteful, that the Jews celebrate this holiday by eating poppy-seed cookies named for a brutal would-be slaughterer of our people, you can also fill them with apricots.

THE LASTING SIGNIFICANCE OF PURIM

The Purim holiday has endured lo these many centuries because it reminds us of a thrilling victory over an evil man who sought to wipe us from the face of the earth. We celebrate our victory because nobody has ever been mean to us again.

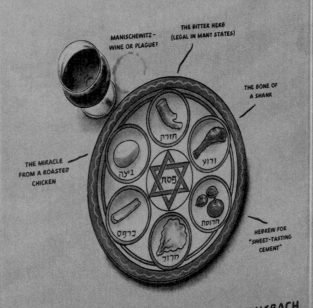

For This We Left Egypt?

A PASSOVER HAGGADAH FOR JEWS AND THOSE WHO LOVE THEM

MANISCHEWITZ – WINE OR PLAGUE?

THE BITTER HERB (LEGAL IN MANY STATES)

THE BONE OF A SHANK

THE MIRACLE FROM A ROASTED CHICKEN

HEBREW FOR "SWEET-TASTING CEMENT"

DAVE BARRY · ALAN ZWEIBEL · ADAM MANSBACH

"THREE OF THE FUNNIEST PEOPLE I'VE EVER CREATED."
—G–D

HOW TO MAKE PERFECT MATZOH BALLS EVERY TIME

Matzoh balls are one of the first prepared foods mentioned by name in the Hebrew Bible, specifically the book of Hamutz, which states: "And they made soup from random chicken parts, and to give it some bulk they added dense spherical dumplings, which in the event of attack could also be used as deadly projectiles."

That is why, to this day, Jews observe significant holidays by making matzoh balls and pretending to enjoy eating them. The ideal matzoh ball is light and fluffy, but many people find these qualities difficult to achieve, because they do not know the Secret. Fortunately for you, we do know the Secret, and we are going to reveal it to you now, on the condition that you will not tell anybody. Promise? Okay!

To make perfect matzoh balls every time, follow these steps exactly:

1. Go to the supermarket.
2. Buy a box of matzoh-ball mix.
3. Read the list of additional ingredients printed on the back of the box.
4. Buy those ingredients.
5. Take all of these items home.
6. Carefully read the directions on the back of the matzoh-ball-mix box.
7. Follow these directions *exactly.*
8. Do NOT modify them in any way.
9. Do NOT change any proportions.
10. Do NOT add or substitute seltzer or baking soda or lard or any other special ingredient that is not mentioned in the directions on the box, but that some friend or relative or other Jewish person claims is the real secret to making perfect matzoh balls.
11. *Just do what it says in the actual directions.*
12. These directions were written by professionals in the matzoh-ball field with vastly more experience than you have, or anybody you know has.
13. These professionals have every reason to want you to have the best possible experience with their product, so you will purchase it again.
14. Their livelihood depends on it!
15. So in their own self-interest they are going to provide you with the best possible recipe.
16. They are not going to deliberately leave out some secret ingredient or technique, without which the finished product would be inferior.

They are not part of some fiendish international matzoh-ball-mix-manufacturer conspiracy to deliberately worsen the outcome for you, their customer.

That's why they go out of their way to give you the optimum recipe, as clearly printed on the box.

So just follow the recipe, okay?

Never mind what your mother's great-aunt Sadie allegedly added to her matzoh balls to make them special.

That woman's matzoh balls had the density of granite.

On the first night of Passover in 1946 your mother's great-uncle Mort bit into one of those things and wound up paying $650 for repairs to his bridgework.

And he got a discount from your mother's great-uncle Sy, who was a dentist.

So what we are saying here is JUST FOLLOW THE FUCKING RECIPE ON THE BOX.

We apologize for our language.

But *sheesh*.

NEXT YEAR IN JERUSALEM

The very last words of the traditional seder are "Next year in Jerusalem." This was always an emotionally significant moment before there was a state of Israel, thereby making this a heartfelt expression of desire to someday return to a Jewish homeland, just as we did when we left Egypt.

Then, after the creation of Israel in 1948, the meaning of the phrase changed to proclaim that maybe next Passover one of the adults at this table will spring for a few plane tickets so we can actually see some of the places we've been praying and singing and getting the shit kicked out of us about all these years.

The phrase does, however, have one glaring oversight. What about those people who already live in Jerusalem? For them to say "Next year in Jerusalem" simply means that they'll be staying put and often leads to family squabbles such as this transcription—as reported on the police blotter page of *The Jerusalem Post* last Passover—between a father and his eleven-year-old son.

FATHER: So that concludes our seder, and we say, next year in Jerusalem.

ASSEMBLED: Next year in Jerusalem.

FATHER: Shlomo, I noticed you didn't say it.

SHLOMO: That's right.

FATHER: Why?

SHLOMO: Because I don't want to be here again next year. It's getting boring.

FATHER: You are calling the holiest city of our people boring?

SHLOMO: Well, yeah. I'd love to see something else for a change. Like the Statue of Liberty or where Charles Lindbergh is buried in Hawaii.

FATHER: Charles Lindbergh! That anti-Semite!

SHLOMO: All I meant was that it would be nice to have a seder in Hawaii.

FATHER: Lindbergh you want to visit instead of celebrating our liberation from bondage here in the center of our people's spiritual heartbeat!

SHLOMO: Hey, calm down, Pop. Your face is turning red.

FATHER: Don't tell me to calm down, you foul emission from another man's loins!

SHLOMO: Another man?

FATHER: That's right! You were adopted, you impudent shithook.

SHLOMO: I was?

FATHER: Oh, look. Now the little Jew hater is starting to cry like Esau did after Jacob stole his birthright. Well, I'll give you something to cry about, you little . . .

SHLOMO: Pop, put down that shank bone!

FATHER: You little . . . you little . . . you . . . you . . .

SHLOMO: Pop! What's going on? Now you're even redder than before . . . !

It was but a matter of minutes before Pop was pronounced dead by the Israeli paramedics. And, in an ironic twist of fate, when a rather harsh Israeli high court found young Shlomo guilty of contributing to the death of his adoptive father, he spent the next ten Passovers in a Jerusalem jail.

TEN REMARKABLE SIMILARITIES
BETWEEN MOSES AND ELVIS

Shortly after President Kennedy was assassinated, historians issued a list of rather uncanny coincidences comparing him to Abraham Lincoln. Such facts as: both of their names had seven letters, Kennedy had an assistant named Lincoln while Lincoln had one named Kennedy, they were both succeeded by vice presidents named Johnson who were born in '08, Lincoln was shot in the head on a Friday in Ford's Theater and Kennedy was shot in the head on a Friday while riding in a Lincoln, which is made by Ford, etc.

As dazzling as some of these are, in 1977, shortly after the death of rock 'n' roll icon Elvis Presley, a conclave of Orthodox rabbis with too much time on their hands saw fit to compile a list of jaw-dropping similarities between Elvis and Moses, who was a rock star in his own right.

1. The names Moses and Elvis both have five letters.

2. Moses had a brother named Aaron; Elvis's middle name was Aaron.

3. Moses left Egypt; Elvis left the building.

4. Moses led the freed Hebrew slaves across the desert; Elvis played Las Vegas, which is in the middle of a desert.

5. Moses used a staff to walk across the Sinai; Elvis had a staff that waited on him at Graceland.

6. Moses delivered the commandments written on stone tablets; Elvis was often stoned from too many prescription tablets.

7. It took Moses forty years to cross the desert; by the time Elvis performed his last concert he had a forty-inch neck.

8. Moses and his fellow slaves lived in a really squalid section of Egypt; Elvis sang "In the Ghetto."

9. Moses parted the Red Sea; Elvis parted from his wife, Priscilla.

10. The Angel of Death passed over Moses's doorway; Elvis passed out before he died on a bathroom floor.

THE BOOK OF JOSHUA

The Book of Joshua is the sixth book in the Hebrew Bible. Yes, we know what you're thinking: "Hey, the Old Testament is called the *Five* Books of Moses! Where in G-d's name did this sixth one come from? What gives? Did Stephen King write it?" We understand your bewilderment. The fact is that this is a bit of a misnomer, because the scriptures that follow the five books are actually historical addenda to the Book of Deuteronomy, so a more accurate name for the sixth book would be along the lines of the Pamphlet of Joshua.

Now that that's out of the way, what follows is the story of Joshua, a stonecutter who lived during the time that the Jews were slaves in Egypt and had a dramatic career change and became a great leader despite his ridiculous haircut, which inspired the naming of the Joshua tree after him.

THE BATTLE OF JERICHO

After the death of Moses, G-d told Joshua to lead the Israelites across the Jordan River to the Promised Land and vowed that He would assure victories in all future battles as long as they obeyed His laws. "As I was with Moses, so I will be with thee. I will not fail thee or forsake thee" (Joshua 1:5).

Joshua, who recognized a good deal when he saw one, sent two spies to Jericho to investigate the territory—sort of like how the New England Patriots have been said to secretly film other NFL teams' practices.

While in Jericho the spies came upon a harlot named Rahab (aka Stormy Rahab), who hid them in her home to ensure their safety from the king, who had heard about Israel's recent successes and was less than thrilled. The flow of the Jordan River temporarily stopped, allowing Joshua and the Israelites, led by a team of priests carrying the Ark of the Covenant, to cross to the other side, where the men were able to prepare for the upcoming battle by performing the prebattle ritual of circumcision.

Now exactly why altering the shape of a soldier's penis was part of this routine rather than, let's say, a hearty prewar breakfast has been the subject of great debate among rabbis through the ages. Some feel a finely sculpted member induces pride and confidence in military men, while others insist that the removal of the foreskin makes the soldiers that much lighter, allowing them to run faster if they should find themselves in retreat.

Either way, Joshua led his army as they fought the battle of Jericho, Jericho, Jericho and the walls came tumbling down.

THE MIRACLE OF JOSHUA

After this victory, Joshua's fame spread throughout the land. Next up was the taking of the city of Ai, where Israelites celebrated afterward by erecting an altar to publicly reaffirm their commitment to G-d and his laws. Yes, Joshua was on a roll, but by far his most dazzling feat was the war where he and his army defended the city of Gibeon against the five armies that were attacking it. During the battle it looked as if the Israelites might indeed win against these overwhelming odds. Then, as the sun began to set, the following happened . . .

> *Then spake Joshua to the Lord in the day*
> *when the Lord delivered up the Amorites*
> *before the children of Israel and he said,*
> *"Sun, stand still." . . . And the sun stood still*
> *until the children of Israel had avenged*
> *themselves upon their enemies.*
> —JOSHUA 10:12

He asked G-d to hold the sun in the sky so he could finish fighting! And G-d did it! The only time in history when a man asked G-d for a favor and G-d obeyed him—except, of course, for that other time, when Sylvester Stallone looked skyward and prayed before shocking the boxing world by winning the heavyweight crown against Apollo Creed in *Rocky II*.

JOSHUA BIDS FAREWELL

From there, the Israelites went on to destroy all the cities in Canaan, as G-d had stipulated. The people of Israel, weary from all this fighting, began to settle in the Promised Land (Joshua 12:1) and divided it up among the twelve tribes. As for a now aging and ailing Joshua, he made a final announcement where he reminded the nation of Israel to obey all G-d's laws, throw away all their idols, and not exchange vows with anyone who wasn't Jewish until their second marriages.

Then he died.

SHAVUOT

Shavuot is one of the lesser-known Jewish holidays—pretty much the way Zeppo and Gummo are the lesser-known Marx brothers.

The word *shavuot* means "weeks," and the holiday marks the conclusion of the counting of the Omer. What is the Omer and why do we count it, you ask? Well, the second day of Passover is the first day of the Omer, and exactly seven weeks later is the last day of the Omer. Get it? No? Well, what if we told you that the Hebrew slaves left Egypt on the second day of Passover and forty-nine days later they received the Torah at the foot of Mount Sinai and that the forty-ninth day is called Shavuot—the holiday commemorating our receiving the Holy Book? Now do you understand? You do? Then perhaps you can tell us how Moses received the Torah forty-nine days into a forty-year trek across the desert yet the rest of that trip and a lot of other events that occurred afterward are written in the Torah. And why were Moses and the Israelites surprised by anything that happened to them when all they had to do was read the Torah and they would've known beforehand what to expect and had plenty of time to prepare?

Just as confounding is the other significance of Shavuot, which is that it is the celebration of wheat harvesting in the land of Israel. Okay, even if we went along with the idea that wheat is worthy of a holiday, why schedule it on the same day we received the Torah? The authors of this book are not farmers (although Adam did major in animal husbandry at the College of the Ozarks), but we stand confident that it takes more than one day to harvest all the wheat in Israel and that another day could have been chosen. So why didn't they? According to Rabbis Mordecai Blitzer (no relation to Wolf) and Rachel Maddow (no relation to Rachel Maddow), this was purposely done as a diversionary tactic so people wouldn't question how Moses, who lived over three thousand years ago, has such white teeth in all his pictures whereas Steve Buscemi's look like the gravel at the bottom of an aquarium.

TISHA B'AV

It is not often that a holiday ceases to be observed simply because it is such a bummer—particularly by a people that has endured so much tribulation, and also invented the concept of humor. But such is the fate of Tisha B'Av, an increasingly obscure day on which we perform rites of deep mourning—the same rites we would perform if a close relative had died—to commemorate the destruction of the two temples in Jerusalem.

Tisha B'Av actually draws its origins from the time when G-d told Moses that because they were insufficiently faithful, the Israelites would not be allowed to enter the Promised Land for forty years— until a generation that had never known slavery came along. "So, like . . . what are we supposed to do, just wait around to die?" Moses is said to have asked. "Let me put it this way," Adonai is said to have responded.

"You could make another Golden Calf, milk it, produce and market a line of Artisanal Golden Calf Brie, wrap it in bacon and lobster jerky, and offer it up as a sacrifice to the Phoenician fertility god Baal, and you wouldn't be in any more trouble than you are right now."

But these ancient tragedies merely scratch the surface of why we choose to spend this day fasting, remembering, and wallowing in grief! As it turns out, a whole bunch of other horrible stuff has also happened on or around Tisha B'Av—the ninth day of the month of Av, which usually falls in late July or early August:

- On Tisha B'Av in 1096, the First Crusade officially kicked off with a festive reception featuring an open cocktail bar from 7 to 9 P.M., followed by the killing of ten thousand Jews.
- On Tisha B'Av in 1290, the king of England ordered the Jews expelled, though luckily they received a warm welcome in nearby France.
- On Tisha B'Av in 1306, the Jews were expelled from France. Luckily, most of them preferred Spain anyway, so they decided to go hang out there instead.
- On Tisha B'Av in 1492, the Jews were expelled from Spain unless they converted. "Converted what?" they asked. "Just leave," said Spain.
- On Tisha B'Av in 1660, in a landlocked Hungarian shtetl hundreds of miles from any body of water, the first recipe for gefilte fish was written.
- On Tisha B'Av in 1956, Mel Gibson was born in Peekskill, New York.
- On Tisha B'Av in 1965, Sandy Koufax surrendered three home runs and the Dodgers lost to the Philadelphia Phillies, 8–1.
- On Tisha B'Av in 1990, one of the authors was expelled from a movie theater in Brookline, Massachusetts, missing the latter two-thirds of the movie *House Party*.
- On Tisha B'Av in 2009, Ivanka Trump converted to Judaism.

SIMCHAT TORAH

Simchat Torah ("Rejoicing of the Torah") is a holiday that marks
the conclusion of the annual cycle of public Torah readings and the
beginning of a new cycle. After the last portion of Deuteronomy is
read, the Torah is scrolled back to its beginning and then the first
portion of Genesis is read. This is very much like finishing a book
that took you a year to read, then immediately starting it all over
again before taking any time off to read something else—like any
of the fine books that the authors of *this* book have written. Really,
would it be so terrible after ending the Torah if Jews took a break
by reading *Go the Fuck to Sleep* before turning their attention back
to the Holy Scriptures?

At the Simchat Torah service, when the ark that houses the Torah is opened, all the scrolls are removed and carried around the

sanctuary in a series of seven circuits. After the last revolution, congregants are encouraged to leave their seats and dance in a joyous celebration that often spills out onto the street.

Just what dances are done while holding the Torah tends to vary with each denomination—as Orthodox congregations tend to prefer livelier dances such as the Twist and the Mashed Potato, Conservatives lean more toward graceful ballroom fare like the waltz and tango, while Reform Jews display a strong penchant for doing the Limbo Rock, with the bar getting surprisingly low despite the fact that they have Torahs lying on their chests.

Children are encouraged to join this celebration as well by carrying Israeli flags, eating all kinds of candy and chocolate treats, and often dancing all the way to their dentist's office, thanks to the cavities they've gotten along the way.

Another custom specific to the Simchat Torah service is that all congregants are invited up to the pulpit for an aliyah—which is the blessing recited just prior to the reading of that week's Torah portion. Now, in smaller temples this is not a problem, especially if it is performed in small groups. But in larger synagogues of upwards of five hundred or even a thousand members, this practice can be rather time consuming as well as costly when those with aliyahs miss work because of the long lines. Which, in turn, can result in longer lines at the unemployment office after those people waiting for an aliyah are fired. Which, in turn, can frustrate those unemployed folks even more because they'll be standing in line instead of looking for new jobs. Which, in turn, could hurt our country's economy because of all those unfilled positions. Which is why the stock market crash of 1929, which caused the Great Depression, can be directly linked to Simchat Torah.

THE HISTORY
OF THE JEWS

THE CREATION STORY

The Creation story is very important in Judaism. If Creation had never taken place, many of the things that we, as Jews, take for granted would not exist. Barbra Streisand is only one example.

The Hebrew Bible tells the story of Creation in the Book of Bereishit, which is not a funny name *at all* even though it ends with "shit." The book opens with G-d creating heaven, earth, light, sea, land, plants, animals, Starbucks, etc. Then G-d creates Adam and gives him dominion over—and this is a direct quote from the Book of Bereishit—"every creeping thing that creepeth on the Earth."

So the Bible clearly states that we, as humans, are the bosses of the animal kingdom. Some animals clearly recognize this. Dogs, for example. Give a dog a command such as "Sit!" and the odds are good that the dog will sit, in recognition of the fact that you have dominion over it, and also that you might be about to give it a treat. Whereas cats will not sit. Cats reject biblical teachings because they are, biologically, the spawn of Satan. Say "Sit!" to a cat and it will just stare at you, thinking about how when you're not looking it's going to urinate in your granola. Beetles are a different story. Say "Sit!" to a beetle and it will not sit, but this is not because it does not respect the Book of Bereishit.* It will not sit because it *can't* sit. Think about it: What would it sit *on*? Beetles don't have butts.† So the beetle is not disrespecting you, although if it did, you could stomp on it, seeing as how you have biblical dominion over "every creeping thing that creepeth on the Earth," which definitely covers beetles.

But getting back to the story of Creation: Chapter 2 of the Book of Bereishit states that after creating Adam, G-d put him in the Garden of Eden, which contained numerous fruit-bearing trees as well as a river that divided into four rivers, one of which was named "Pishon," which is also not a funny name, especially for a river. G-d told Adam that he could eat from any of the trees *except* the tree of knowledge. G-d also decided to provide Adam with what the Book of Bereishit calls a "helpmeet," so he put Adam to sleep, took one of his ribs, and made it into Eve, an event known to theologians as the First Cloning. When they were first created, Adam and Eve were both naked. The Book of Bereishit does not specifically state that G-d was also naked, but we like to think He was.

At this point in the story the serpent showed up and asked Eve if there was any specific tree in the Garden of Eden that G-d had told her and Adam not to eat from.

To which Eve replied, "JESUS CHRIST A TALKING SNAKE."

No, we're kidding. Back then nobody had heard of Jesus Christ. Eve replied that G-d had told her and Adam not to eat from the tree of knowledge, and the serpent was like: *Really,* girlfriend? So the

---

* Especially not if it's . . . a *dung* beetle. Get it? Ha ha!

† As far as we know.

serpent talked Eve into eating fruit from the tree of knowledge, and Eve—who apparently had a poor understanding of the term "help-meet"—talked Adam into eating some.

Hoo boy.

Suddenly Adam and Eve realized they were naked, and—again we quote directly from the Book of Bereishit—"they sewed fig leaves together and made themselves girdles."

This raises a number of questions:

- If Adam and Eve had not previously been aware that they were naked, how did they suddenly know how to make clothes?
- What did they use to sew the fig leaves?
- Did there just happen to be a needle and thread lying around the previously garment-free Garden of Eden?
- And why did they make girdles?
- Had they been snacking on the tree of carbohydrates?

The Book of Bereishit does not address these questions. What it does say is that when G-d found out that Adam and Eve had eaten from the tree of knowledge, he was seriously p.o.'d. He kicked Adam and Eve out of the Garden of Eden and condemned them to a life of toil and pain, and mankind has been suffering ever since. And all because of a snake. Which is yet another reason why Jews are opposed to camping.

THE EIGHTH DAY

To review, according to Genesis, this is how G-d spent the week that he created everything.

Day 1—Night and Day

Day 2—The Sky and the Sea

Day 3—Land and Vegetation

Day 4—The Stars, the Sun, and the Moon

Day 5—Sea Creatures and Birds

Day 6—Animals and Humans

Day 7—Rest

Yes, a full week is certainly deserving of a day of relaxation.

But what about the next day? The eighth day of the world's existence. When the Lord awakened, fully rested, with nothing to do. When all he created was up and running and enjoying the life he had given it.

"Now what?" he wondered aloud. "What shall *I* do?"

And the Lord kept repeating this while pacing and twiddling his Almighty thumbs.

"What shall *I* do? What shall *I* do?"

And then it struck him.

"Oh, I know. I'll visit Adam and Eve."

So G-d went down to the Garden of Eden, where he came upon the first two humans, who were walking around familiarizing themselves with their new surroundings.

"And those white splotches are called bird shit," said Adam.

"Boy, there sure is a lot of bird shit here in the Garden of Eden," said Eve. "Now, what about those feathered things that are flying around?"

"Those are the birds that the shit is dropping out of."

"Oh . . ."

"Boo!" said the Lord, jumping out from behind a tree. "Happy to see me?"

"Oh, hi, G-d," said Adam rather nonchalantly.

"Good morning, Lord," Eve said politely before turning her attention back to the tour her new husband was giving her. "And that long fleshy thing that's wiggling back and forth?"

"My penis?" asked Adam.

"No, that one over there."

"Oh, that's a koi. It's a kind of fish," answered Adam with a hint of disappointment.

"So what are you guys up to?" asked G-d.

"Just taking in the sights," said Adam, shaking his head.

"Anything I can help you with? Any questions that need answering?" asked G-d.

"No, we're cool," said Eve.

"But thanks for the offer," said Adam. "Now, as long as we're on the subject," he said to Eve, "the penis is a most fascinating instrument because . . ."

"Instrument?"

"Yes, because it can be played in oh so many ways . . ."

"Mind if I join you?" asked G-d.

"We're fine!" snapped Adam with just a hint of an attitude.

"My Lord, Lord," said Eve. "Can't you see we're doing fine by ourselves?"

"But you wouldn't even exist to be doing so damn fine if it weren't for me," argued G-d in a tone matching her apparent ire. "I'm the one who made you. In my own image, my I add?"

"Yeah, yeah, and we appreciate it," Adam shot back. "But now it's time to for us to start exercising some of that free will you gave us."

"Fine. But what about me?" asked G-d.

"What *about* you?" asked Eve. "Isn't it time for us to start living our lives? To explore and have our own experiences?"

"Even if it means making our own mistakes but learning from them?" added Adam.

"But I'm bored!" the Lord whined. "I'm bored! I'm bored! I'm bored!" he wailed, jumping up and down.

"Boy, His actions are highly unattractive," Adam whispered to Eve.

"Hardly becoming of a Supreme Being," Eve whispered back.

"It's not fair! Everything and everyone else goes off and leaves me alone! Is that fair? Is that fair?" G-d repeated before falling to the ground and flailing his outstretched arms and legs, not unlike the amphibians he had created only three days earlier.

"What should we do?" asked Adam, covering his mouth with a fig so his lips could not be read by the Lord, who had now flipped over onto his back.

"I can't listen to this howling much longer."

"Well, we can't just move on and leave him here, can we?"

Adam looked down at the Lord, whose countenance was turning crimson and who was gasping for the very air he created on the first day.

"No, I guess not," said Eve, in what the rabbis agree was the first lament.

" . . . Would you like to accompany us on our walk, dear Lord?"

"You sure I won't be imposing?"

"Yeah, yeah, we're sure," said Adam.

"Eve . . . ?" asked the Lord, his lower lip quivering just a bit.

"Fine," she answered in a tone that sounded more like "I would prefer to have severe labor pains while bearing a child."

"Great!" said G-d, jumping to his feet and smiling before joining the extremely unhappy Adam and Eve on their walk through the Garden of Eden.

And so it was that on the eighth day, the Lord created whining, the tantrum, and the guilt trip.

THE ORIGINS OF JUDAISM

The very first Jew was a man named Abram, who was born during the Bronze Age in the Mesopotamian city of Ur (motto: "Ur Going to Like It Here!").

The Book of Genesis says that when Abram was seventy-five years old, the Lord came to him in a vision, which was like an ancient version of Skype, and told Abram that he was going to be the father of many nations. At the time Abram was a career nomad, so this was a major promotion.

Following the Lord's instructions, Abram and his wife, Sarai, who at sixty-five was also no spring chicken, went to Canaan, where they stayed for ten years, during which time they did not get any younger. Then the Lord came to Abram in another vision and again told him that he was going to be the father of nations. Abram was eighty-five and Sarai was seventy-five, and they still had no children, so Abram was starting to wonder if there was some kind of technical difficulty that was causing him to receive somebody else's visions.

At this point Sarai—they don't make them like her anymore—suggested to Abram that since she couldn't bear children, he should get together with her Egyptian slave girl, Hagar. The Book of Genesis says—and if you don't think the Bible has a sense of humor, check out this line—"And Abram listened to the voice of Sarai." Ha ha! We BET he did. So he and Hagar got together, and she gave birth to a son, Ishmael, whose main accomplishment after that as far as we can tell was dying at age 137. (Back then people lived much longer than today because their diet consisted mainly of bark.)

Thirteen years later, when Abram was ninety-nine, the Lord *again* appeared to him in a vision to inform him—stop us if you have heard this—that he was going to be a father of many nations. The Lord further stated that Abram and Sarai were going to have a son together, which Abram thought was pretty funny, as this was roughly four thousand years before the invention of Viagra. But the Lord was serious this time. He said he was giving Abram and Sarai new names, namely Abraham and Sarah. (The Lord considered calling them Irving and Sadie, but decided that sounded too Jewish.)

The Lord also said that, as a sign of the covenant between Abraham and Himself, Abraham and all the males in his household had to be circumcised. And Abraham said, "How about instead we just shake hands?" But the Lord had a bee in His bonnet about foreskin removal. He further insisted that all Abraham's future male descendants, at eight days old, had to be circumcised in a ritual ceremony followed by deli platters. And so Abraham immediately circumcised all the males in his household himself, and we can only imagine what a fun day THAT was.

But it was totally worth it because the next year, as the Lord had promised, Abraham and Sarah had a son, Isaac. After that everything was fine for several years, at which point the Lord, out of the blue, told Abraham to take Isaac to a mountain and *sacrifice him as a burnt offering.* If the Book of Genesis finds it in any way odd that the Lord, after all those years of promises about being the father of nations, suddenly tells this hundred-plus-year-old man to turn his son into a human shish kebab, the Book of Genesis remains mum. It merely states that Abraham took Isaac on a three-day camping trip into the mountains, tied him up, laid him on top of some firewood, and got ready to stab him with a knife.

Fortunately, just then the angel of the Lord grabbed Abraham's hand and said "Kidding! KIDDING!" Turns out it was all just a test to see if Abraham was obedient to the Lord, who yet *again* told Abraham that he would be the father of many etc. And indeed, through Isaac, Abraham had numerous descendants, although to this very day Jews are highly suspicious of camping.

DISCUSSION QUESTIONS FOR "THE ORIGINS OF JUDAISM"

- Some believe that the remarkable resiliency of Judaism owes to its double founding, first as a people and then as a religion, first by Abraham and then by Moses, first by a father and then by a lawgiver. Do you agree or disagree? Why or why not? How or how not? When or when not?
- As long as the Lord was hooking Abraham up with all these super sex powers, why didn't he just do the same for Sarah? Wouldn't that have been simpler? Stage a play of no more than twenty minutes that answers these questions.

THE FIRST JEWISH COMEDIAN

The Marx Brothers. Jack Benny. Carl Reiner. Mel Brooks. Billy Crystal. Joan Rivers. Larry David. Sarah Silverman. Jerry Seinfeld. What do all these funny people have in common? For those of you who said they are all left-handed Asian Americans we are at a total loss for a dignified response, though we do pray for your souls. But if your answer was that they are all Jewish, you would be right.

Throughout the annals of humor, whether it be the written words of Sholem Aleichem and Dorothy Parker, the stage plays of George S. Kaufman and Neil Simon, the comedy routines of Mike Nichols and Elaine May, the television shows of Carl Reiner and Lorne Michaels, the films of Woody Allen and Judd Apatow—Jews have had an influence in this field that is vastly disproportionate to our percentage of the population.

Not unlike how sometimes there are too many peanuts in an order of kung pao chicken.

Why are Jews so funny? It is an oft-asked question for which there are only theories, the most popular being that we've needed a sense of humor in order to survive the oppression we've endured and the second most popular being that we just seem funny compared to most other religions that take themselves so fucking seriously.

When did this start? According to the Old Testament, it began at the very beginning of our religion, in the book of Genesis, when G-d said to Abraham, "Avram, you are a laugh riot." And the claim that the very first Jew was also the very first Jewish comedian was further substantiated in 1997 when archaeologists excavating in the Cave of Machpelah, where Abraham and his wife Sarah are buried, deciphered the ancient engravings on the cave's wall and determined them to be the following monologue written and delivered by the patriarch of our faith.

"How is everyone tonight? *(to a man)* Tired from your day in the fields and *(to a woman)* from washing his loincloths in the Jordan River? Hi, I'm Abraham, also known as the first Jew, also known as the first man to circumcise himself to show his devotion to G-d. *(anticipate applause)* Thank you, although I must say that when the Lord first commanded it I asked if I could show my devotion by letting him win when we play cards . . . But no, the Almighty wanted my foreskin—although my now Jewish penis is so small that it was technically a threeskin. *(anticipate groans)* Oh, you're groaning? Well, imagine how my wife Sarah groaned on our wedding night when she discovered that she had just married a two-hundred-pound pull cart with a two-inch string . . . Sarah was ninety years old when she gave birth to our son Isaac. You hear me? Ninety! Her vagina was so dry that when Isaac emerged from that birth canal there were rope burns on his body . . . I'm not kidding. Sarah is so dry that she breastfed Isaac powdered milk . . . *(off of big laugh)* It's ironic that you're laughing, since we named our son Isaac because in Hebrew it means 'laugh'—which is what Sarah did when she found out she was pregnant. Few people know we came this close to naming our son 'Schmuck,' which is what I felt like when they handed me the hospital bill! . . . Good night everyone, I'll be here all week! *(bow, wave to the audience, leave the stage, go back to the dressing room, and put more bandages on your penis)*"

THE STORY OF ISAAC

Isaac was the son of Abraham and Sarah. It is said that when she informed her one-hundred-year-old husband of her pregnancy he suggested the name Sagebrush in honor of Sarah's uterus, which, at this point in her life, resembled a ghost town. But like all Jewish husbands who followed for the next fifty-seven hundred years, he let her have her way and retreated to the man cave section of the cave they lived in.

Like any child with really old parents, Isaac was embarrassed by their advanced ages. The way Abraham always had a little wet spot on the front of his robes thanks to the ragged condition of his century-old prostate, or how his friends secretly referred to Sarah as a MILF (Mother I'd Like to Fossilize), or how he was the object of merciless scorn from friends whose much younger parents had died of old age while Abraham and Sarah kept chugging along.

But probably—no, make that most definitely—the biggest gripe Isaac had was when his dad took him to Mount Moriah, tied him to a stake, and was about to impale him with a rather large knife when a messenger of G-d interrupted him. What follows is the dialogue that rabbis tell us took place between Isaac and his father during the ride home afterward.

ISAAC: What the hell was that all about?

ABRAHAM: G-d told me I should . . .

ISAAC: You call this good parenting?

ABRAHAM: The Lord was testing my faith . . .

ISAAC: I'm your child, damn it!

ABRAHAM: Hey, I ended up not stabbing you . . .

ISAAC: Because someone else stopped you . . .

ABRAHAM: And I sacrificed that ram instead . . .

ISAAC: Who gives a shit about that ram?

ABRAHAM: Please watch your language, son . . .

ISAAC: Don't you dare call me son!

ABRAHAM: But . . .

ISAAC: You swapped me out for a fucking ram!

ABRAHAM: . . . Ike?

ISAAC: What?

ABRAHAM: Do me a favor and don't tell your mother about this?

ISAAC: (Mimicking) Don't tell your mother, don't tell your mother. Boy, you're a wimpy patriarch!

Eventually, after Abraham and Sarah died suddenly at the ages of 175 and 127, respectively, Isaac was a seventy-four-year-old orphan who inherited the family's thriving business (farming, as well as a chain of lamb repair shops) and had two sons with his wife, Rebekah. Their names were Jacob and Esau, and their sibling rivalry, while not as dramatic as that of Cain and Abel, who reduced Adam and Eve's holiday card featuring their children by 50 percent, was biblically noteworthy in its own way.

Isaac was now one hundred years old, blind, and ready to pass on the family business, with the birthright (the larger share) designated for the older son, Esau. So he told Esau to go hunt some wild game for a delicious dinner and that after they ate he'd give him his blessing. But Rebekah, who favored her younger son, told Jacob to go out and quickly bring back two fine goats so she could prepare Isaac's favorite dinner (that's right, Isaac really enjoyed a delicious goat), then Jacob could serve the goat to his blind father and get the blessing meant for Esau.

"But Esau is hairier than I am," said Jacob. "If he touches me he'll surely know that I am not my brother." So before Jacob served his blind father the delicious dinner, Rebekah covered his arms and the back of his neck with the skins of the goats and tricked Isaac, after he touched him, into giving Jacob his blessing.

As a result, the name Jacob came to mean "deceive," Esau never sent Rebekah a card on Mother's Day, and Isaac remained blind until he died at the age of 180.

THE KINGS OF ISRAEL: THE FIRST TEMPLE

For the first couple of centuries after the Israelites entered the land of Canaan, they were a loose assortment of tribes without any central government, possibly since central government—in the form of a schmucktacular pharaoh so thick-headed that millions of frogs falling out of the skies was not enough to convince him to reconsider his human rights policies—had gone poorly for them in the past.

Instead, each Israelite tribe just did its own thing, with some transitioning from a nomadic to an agricultural society, and others concentrating on bowling. This went on for about two weeks, at which point the Israelites were attacked by the Philistines, the Philactics, the Jets, the Savage Skulls, the Raymond Avenue Crips, the Rotarians, and the Knights of Ren.

"This sucks," Schmuel, of the tribe of Reuben, was heard to remark. "If we don't unite under a single leader, this period of chaos that began roughly in 1200 B.C.E. shall surely continue until roughly 1020 B.C.E."

And indeed, Schmuel's words proved prescient, for it was in 1020 B.C.E. (roughly) that the tribes, tired of getting their lunch eaten by every marauding gang and Girl Scout troop in the greater Canaan area, complained to G-d and demanded a strong government ruled by a single king.

G-D CHOOSES SAUL

G-d was not used to weighing in on municipal issues, but the tribes were hopelessly mired in petty squabbling, and it was clear they could no more select their own king than construct a nuclear warhead. Only a monarch chosen by G-d could transcend both partisan bickering and the fundamental stupidity of the ancient Israelites' procedure for selecting a leader, which was based on the Electoral College.

And so G-d reached out his mighty hand and fingered Saul for the job. This was very much a surprise to Saul, who had been wandering around in search of his father's lost donkeys when the prophet Samuel approached and told him that he had been chosen as king.

"Have you seen my donkeys, though?" Saul responded.

Samuel ignored the question and proceeded to anoint him with oil. "Why the oil?" asked Saul, but Samuel just shrugged and kept on anointing. "Is this really necessary?" Saul protested. "This oil smells used."

SAUL POOPS THE BED

Things went downhill from there. Saul's reign was marked by constant war with the Philistines, and he fell into a deep depression. It didn't help that his son-in-law, David, was always playing the freaking harp and making up beautiful, tender songs—which makes him sound like a bit of a candy-ass until you consider the fact that he also killed a giant by slingshotting a rock directly into his testicles, saving the Israelites and inadvertently inventing slapstick comedy at the same time.

Tensions escalated between Saul and David and, as often happens between in-laws, Saul tried to have David killed on several occasions, employing the forebears of the assassins the CIA would later hire to kill Fidel Castro. Eventually, David grew weary of declining poisoned cigars and avoiding exploding seashells. He put together an army of mercenaries and left to fight the Philistines on his own, in an episode of Jewish history that is just crying out for a film adaptation.

Saul, meanwhile, was surrounded by enemies and desperate for Samuel's advice. The only problem was that Samuel was no longer alive, so Saul asked the Witch of Endor* to raise him from the dead. Even the Witch of Endor knew this was a big no-no—she mostly confined herself to wearing pants and skirts at the same time and having loud conversations about her dreams in crowded cafés, like the witches of today—but Saul insisted.

Samuel's spirit rose and spoke to Saul, asking, "Why hast thou disturbed me?"

"I still can't find those donkeys," Saul replied, at which point Samuel informed him that G-d was displeased with his whining and necromancy, and had appointed David to take his place.

"Why did He choose me to begin with when I'm clearly a total incompetent?" Saul asked, but Samuel's spirit was already fading away. "This raising of the dead has manifold teleological implications we haven't even begun to unpack!" Saul bellowed into the void, but there was no response, so he went and died in a battle and soon afterward David took over as king.

---

* Different Endor.

DAVID: MORE INTERESTING THAN SAUL

David was a much better king than Saul, and his reign ushered in an era of . . . well, an era of constant warfare much like Saul's, except that under David the Israelites started to win and expand their territory. This left David plenty of time to fall in love with married women.

One day, David was standing on the roof of his palace, possibly smoking a joint,* when he espied Bathsheba taking a bath. Acting with the kind of swift, decisive leadership that had made him such a military juggernaut, David proceeded to get her pregnant later that afternoon. Then, in a move so sleazy that you kind of have to respect it, he had her husband, Uriah the Hittite, called back from his army posting, in the hopes that Uriah and Bathsheba would lie together and Uriah would think the kid was his.

But Uriah wouldn't come,† so instead David ordered him to the front lines, and Uriah was promptly killed, and David was like, "Oh, what a tragedy, he was a brave and noble man, and as your king it is incumbent upon me to provide whatever small comfort I can, such as marrying the widow." And then he married Bathsheba. To be fair, he had eight other wives at the time, so this wasn't as big a deal as you might think.

G-d was not pleased with any of this, and he sent Nathan the prophet to reprimand David. Up until this point, nobody had ever taken Nathan the prophet seriously, because they considered Nathan to be a silly name for a prophet, but when Nathan scolded David he was remorseful and G-d forgave him, except for the part where he also cursed his house and decreed that his son would rebel against him.

---

* Perfectly legal at the time, and anyway he was the king.
† Back home. He wouldn't come back home.

DAVID'S SON REBELS AGAINST HIM

This would be Absalom. He eventually died in the ensuing civil war, which was upsetting for David but also gave us the great William Faulkner novel *Absalom, Absalom!**

With David's favorite son† dead, the question of who would be the next heir led to another war, but eventually Bathsheba convinced David that it should be her son Solomon.

SOLOMON

Solomon ruled for forty years, and his wisdom, wealth, and writings were almost as legendary as the fact that he had seven hundred wives and three hundred concubines, each of whom cooked him a delicious dinner every day in the hopes that he might dine with her that night—the only instance in recorded history of Jewish women allowing food to go to waste.

Perhaps the best-known story about Solomon's wisdom is the Judgment of Solomon, in which two women came to him, each claiming to be the mother of the same child. Solomon ordered the child cut in half and shared between the two. One woman immediately renounced her claim. Solomon declared her the mother and awarded her the larger half of the child.

Solomon also fulfilled his father's ambition of building the First Temple in Jerusalem, to house the Ark of the Covenant until such time as archaeologist Indiana Jones could deliver it to a cavernous U.S. government warehouse. To build the temple Solomon conscripted his people into forced labor, while he busied himself by having an affair with the Queen of Sheba (fact), siring Menelik I, the first king in a three-thousand-year Ethiopian dynasty (generally

---

* Which, if we're being honest, we have not actually read.
† Absalom.

agreed upon), and possibly using a magic ring called the Seal of Solomon to control demons and animals (contested).

The minute Solomon died, ten of the twelve Israelite tribes decided it was now the weekend and stopped working, and when his son Rehoboam insisted that they keep building, war broke out and the kingdom split into two: the Northern (Israelite) Kingdom and the Southern (Judean) Kingdom. These were located in the north and the south, respectively.

THE TWO KINGDOMS

Both kingdoms were a mess for the next couple hundred years, poorly ruled and impossible to find a decent sandwich in, but the Northern Kingdom also made the fatal mistake of deciding to stop paying protection money to the Assyrians—who, like Don Fabrizio Fanucci in *The G-dfather Part II*, just wanted to wet their beaks. But there was no young Vito Corleone among the men of the Northern Kingdom, no artfully loosened hallway lightbulb or jamming of gun parts down a succession of chimneys. Instead, the Assyrians smashed the Israelite army to bits in 722 B.C.E. and deported the ten (formerly twelve) tribes of Israel, which would henceforth be known as

THE LOST TRIBES OF ISRAEL

There has been much speculation as to what became of these tribes. Some scholars say they became the Native Americans, the Eskimo, the Irish, the Halal Guys, the Drama Club, Ben & Jerry, Goldman Sachs, the Hair Club for Men, the Jackson 5, and so on. Others say they merely assimilated into Assyrian culture, but those scholars are rarely invited to parties.

THE TEMPLE FALLS

After a bunch of invasions and wars that frankly we are in no mood
to recount in full because we are eager to get back to writing circumcision jokes, the Babylonians overcame the Assyrians and then
beat Egypt 3–1 on penalty kicks to take control of the Southern
Kingdom. At first, the Babylonian king Nebuchadnezzar merely
taxed the Israelites, but then the Israelite puppet king Zedekiah
made a crack about how a king with a name that long must be com-
pensating for something, and Nebuchadnezzar besieged Jerusalem,
put out Zedekiah's eyes, ripped up his stock portfolio, slapped his
favorite camel, and burned down the temple—bringing an end, at
long last, to this chapter.

THE SECOND TEMPLE

After Nebuchadnezzar sacked the temple at the end of the previous chapter, two things happened. First, the king announced that he would henceforth be known as "Chad." And second, for the first time in centuries, there were now more Jews living in exile than in Judea.

THE BABYLONIAN EXILE: KINDA SWEET

Most Jews at that time lived in Babylon, and after the initial shock of having to leave their homes wore off, they were almost obnoxiously happy about it, like San Franciscans who get priced out of the Bay Area and move to Portland. They nattered on and on about how you could own land (try doing *that* back home), practice Judaism, and eat at a different farm-to-table restaurant every night of the week. Sure, it was rainier than Judea, but also Judea wasn't really Judea anymore—it was so full of rich tech assholes now, and flush with money from the irrigation boom.

In 539 B.C.E., Cyrus of Persia conquered Babylonia. As monarchs went, Cyrus was super chill, and he told the Jews that they were free to go back to Judea and rebuild the temple, if they felt like it. But after fifty years in Babylon—which was just such a more *livable* place, with such great produce and so many craft breweries—the Jews were not exactly falling all over themselves to go pay Judea rents again, so only a handful left. And frankly, they were the kind that the other Babylonian Jews were not at all sorry to see go.

HELLENIZATION

The Second Temple was built, and for a couple hundred years everything was pretty good, first under the tolerant Persian government and then under the Greeks, who conquered the Persians in 332 B.C.E. In fact, things were so good that many Jews spoke only Greek and became thoroughly "Hellenized" into a culture that prized things like art, philosophy, beauty, pleasure, and wrestling in the nude. Naturally, there was tension between those who felt that the Jews ought not to stray from the path of being nebbishy, disheveled dorks who thought primarily about religious law, and those who felt that with a modest workout regimen and a few painting classes they could be just as vapid and narcissistic as the Greeks.

Eventually, a middle ground was forged: the Jews would continue to forgo exercise, but they would become sex crazed and write philosophical novels about it. To celebrate this accord, the Torah was translated into Greek for the first time. Legend has it that seventy scholars, each one working in isolation, produced the exact same translation. This would be far more impressive if that translation were not littered with thousands of errors.

A JERK EMPEROR FUCKS EVERYTHING UP

All this peace and happiness came crashing to a halt when a neurotic asshat named Antiochus came to power. Abandoning the "live and let live" philosophy of his predecessors in favor of "assimilate or die," he taxed and restricted the Jews, even going so far as to auction off the role of high priest to the highest bidder as if it were a mere U.S. ambassadorship. This led to the rebellion of the Maccabees, which you can read all about in the Chanukah chapter of this book, or in a reputable source. It ended with a Jew, Simeon Maccabee, on the throne for the first time in 175 years, ushering in a hundred-year Hasmonean dynasty that was the equal of any that had come before it in terms of pure shittiness.

THE PHARISEES VS. THE SADDUCEES VS. THE ESSENES

With a Jew in power, the Jewish people were finally free to form a number of parties that hated each other and destroy themselves from within. On one side you had the Sadducees, or "Temple Cult." These dudes followed Simeon, and they were basically like, "Now that we have a temple again, let's hang out here all the time and sacrifice some animals! Maybe *all* the animals!" You know that one friend of yours who just loves to barbecue, and when he really gets going on the first warm day of spring, there's nothing he won't throw on the grill and no way to get him to step away from it, even if one of his kids is having a grand mal seizure? Imagine that guy as a political party, and you've got the Sadducees.

This was all a little much for the Essenes, who split off and became recluses and probably wrote the Dead Sea Scrolls. You know that one friend of yours who turned out to be the Unabomber? That guy is the Essenes.

Then you had the Pharisees, who believed in the Oral Torah, which they claimed was received by Moses (possibly after the supply of large flat stone tablets atop Mount Sinai had been exhausted) and which later became the basis for the Talmud. They were more interested in having personal relationships to G-d than in setting animals on fire, and they encouraged Jews to worship and study To-rah privately, instead of investing everything in the temple and its priests. You know whom that pissed off? The temple and its priests. Sadducee-supported rulers killed thousands of Pharisees in the years to come, but the Pharisees' decentralized model of worship and study would help Judaism survive when it turned out that ev-erybody else would also try to kill us in the years to come.

MORE HORRIBLE THINGS HAPPEN

Eventually, the Hasmonean dynasty collapsed, and various foreign rulers took a shot at maintaining some sort of equilibrium between the Pharisees and Sadducees—usually by screwing them both over and putting their own people in charge. Alexander the Great's widow Salome came along, made her son Hyrcanus II the high priest, and then, shortsightedly, died. Then her younger son—whose name we can't remember right now but trust us, it doesn't really matter—overthrew his brother with the help of the Sadducees, and even-tually the whole thing turned into such a big dumb sandbox fight between the brothers that they had to call in the Roman general Pompey to settle it. Which he did by dumping them both and mak-ing Judea a vassal state of Rome.

HEROD AND STUFF

Fast forward a few decades and you end up with a guy named Herod governing Judea on behalf of Rome. For the first time in a century, it wasn't about which Jewish faction the ruler supported, because Herod hated everybody and frequently killed family members he suspected might want to usurp him. But like many sociopaths drawn to politics, Herod was good at building things. He turned the Second Temple into an architectural masterpiece, constructed the desert fortress of Masada, and left behind a Judea that was strong on infrastructure and a hot mess in virtually every other way.

Herod's four sons attempted to calm things down by having a bloody four-way war for control of the land. Eventually, Rome gave them each a piece of land, then brought in corrupt governors to control each territory. Among these were Herod Antipas, who had John the Baptist beheaded, and Pontius Pilate, whose name may be familiar to you from the 1992 Delfeayo Marsalis album *Pontius Pilate's Decision*.

Throughout this period, false prophets and fake descendants of King David were popping up every five minutes. The aristocratic, priestly Sadducees and the poorer, humbler Pharisees were sparring over everything from philosophy to control of the temple compound to whether it was okay to put celery in a potato salad. Most Jews, meanwhile, were subsistence farmers getting screwed over by mile-high Roman taxes.

Even when all the tribes finally banded together and went to war with Rome in 66 C.E., the Jewish factions couldn't stop attacking each other long enough to fight their actual enemy. This made it relatively easy for Titus, the new Roman emperor, to conquer Jerusalem, destroy the temple, and march the Jewish armies back to Rome—a breezy fifteen hundred miles away—as prisoners and slaves.

By the time the last revolts petered out in 135 C.E., the Jews were forbidden to live in Jerusalem. Judea was now called Palestine, and Jews who wanted to live there—which few did—had to pay a tax. No temple meant no high priest, and thus it was the Pharisees' model of Judaism-on-the-go that won out, with its newfangled "rabbi" concept. All in all, the Jews were stepping into the new millennium without a pot to piss in, a window to throw it out of, or a priest to recite the prayer for piss-pot-throwing.

THE THIRD TEMPLE

Shortly after the destruction of the Second Temple, three religious Jews and their rabbi sat on top of the pile of rubble with a lot of extra time on their hands.

"I should be praying now," said one of them.

"Me, too. But where?" said another.

"In a temple," said still another.

"No shit," said the one of them. "But we don't have a temple anymore."

"We're sitting on what's left of it," said the another.

"These jagged rocks are hurting my ass," said the still another.

"I kind of like that feeling," mused the another, who suddenly felt the need to clarify when he realized the others were now staring at him. "But still, I'd much rather have a temple than a sharp object in my rectum. Truly. No comparison."

As soon as the others stopped rolling their eyes, shaking their heads, and muttering words like "Weirdo" and "What the hell?" under their breath, the conversation got back to the original subject.

"Maybe we should build a new temple," suggested the first Jew.

"What's the point?" asked Rabbi Chachacha—who had been silent up till now, as he considered the entire situation to be futile. "I mean, we built two temples and both were destroyed. So why erect a third if that will eventually be reduced to shards and fragments as well?"

This unnerved the others, as they had always looked to their spiritual leader to provide a positive spin no matter how bleak things appeared. Like when he told his congregation that the epidemic of hoof-and-mouth disease that wiped out virtually all the livestock in Judea was actually a blessing in disguise because "it will be refreshing to start anew with a herd of cattle that have squeaky clean hooves and mint-scented breath."

But this time, the ordinarily "kiddush cup is half-full" rabbi was morose—a word, for those of you who remember your SAT vocabulary flash cards, that means incredibly sad and gloom filled.

"Maybe our people are just not meant to have a house of worship," he lamented. "Not unlike how some folks are not meant to wear prayer shawls with horizontal stripes because it makes them look paunchy."

But the others were of no mind to indulge his pessimism and made their feelings known.

"Horrible analogy, Rabbi!"

"We need a place to pray!"

"I like being a congregant!"

"Me, too. But how can we be congregants if there's no place to congregate?"

"And if there's no place to congregate we can't have a congregation!"

"Two, four, six, eight, we need a place to congregate!" they all started cheering over and over again until the rabbi had no choice but to respond.

"Okay, okay, I get it!" he shouted. "But we have to be smart about this because I don't think any of us can endure another heartbreak."

"Smart about this? How so?" asked the one of them.

"Is it possible to construct an indestructible temple?" asked the another.

"I can't imagine how," answered the still another. "The first two temples were made of brick and mortar but they went down faster than one of those two-kopek whores that were at Ezekiel's bachelor party."

"Ezekiel got married?" asked the first one.

"He had a bachelor party with two-kopek whores?" asked the another.

"Why wasn't I invited?" wondered the still another.

"Were you invited, Rabbi?"

"Ah, yes, but I didn't go. I swear."

"I'm confused," said the first one. "Was there more than one whore who each charged two kopeks or were there two whores who each charged one kopek?"

"I have no idea . . . ," the still another started to say.

"There were many whores who each charged two kopeks . . . or so I was told," said the rabbi, who was starting to sweat, just a little. "But we are getting off the subject of our new temple, are we not?"

"Yes. We were talking about how to build a temple that would be immune from enemy attack," the first one reminded them.

"True, but we also said that it would be impossible to build such a structure," said the another.

Again they were thrown into silent despair until the rabbi spoke up.

" . . . We can disguise our new temple."

"Disguise it?"

"What does that mean, O Learned One?"

"Well," offered the rabbi gingerly, as if treading on thin ice, "we can build a temple that looks like something else so it won't be recognizable."

The others looked at him, not quite understanding. So he continued. "Like, for example—and this is only an example, mind you—if a prominent man wanted to attend, let's say, a bachelor party he really shouldn't be at, he could, I imagine, dress like a Roman centurion with full body armor, codpiece, and a helmet to avoid detection."

"Sure."

"Makes sense."

"Tell us more, dear, dear Rabbi."

"All I'm suggesting is that we build an innocuous place like a restaurant or a bowling center* that we secretly use as a shul so the Philistines or the Romans or whoever hates our guts in the future will never find us praying in it—just like I pray that the identity of the individual in that hypothetical situation I just told you about is not discovered because he has a family and a revered standing in the community."

"What a great idea!"

"Genius!"

"Let's start building a secret building!"

So, inspired by the rabbi's words, the Jews jubilantly constructed the Third Temple, which may very well be standing to this day but we can't be sure because no one knows which building it is.

---

* For those of you who've got your loincloths in a twist thinking that bowling did not exist at this time, just calm the hell down and direct your outrage elsewhere—as the Second Temple was destroyed in 70 C.E., while archaeologists have unearthed evidence that bowling existed in Egypt as far back as 3200 B.C.E. Okay? Jesus!

THE TALMUD

While the Torah is considered to be the Jewish people's written law, the Talmud is its oral interpretation, although it, too, is written lest we forget what the rabbis were screaming about while disagreeing about the Bible's meaning.

For example, the Torah states that you should "Honor thy father and thy mother" but doesn't mention exactly how you should display that respect. Bowing? Saluting? Allowing Dad to win at Words with Friends even if he never completed high school and finds it easier to take apart a car's engine than spell the word "engine"?

Rituals such as putting on tefillin are commanded, but exactly just how they should be worn is not described. So it's the Talmud that tells us that they should be worn on the head and left arm and not around the thighs to tether partners together during a three-legged race, as originally thought.

Even when it comes to the practice of circumcision, the Torah neglects to specify the penis as the targeted organ, which explains why Abraham also removed one of his kidneys.

TALMUDIC METHOD

The Talmudic method therefore is one characterized by heated debate and, at times, contentious argument among the sages in their attempt for clarification of the tersely written law. Talmudic rabbi Abraham Chhhh, who for decades unsuccessfully argued that the Torah meant for the holiday to be called Chhhhanukah, recounted in his spectacularly mean-spirited memoir "Fucccch You" a discussion about what G-d meant in the fourth commandment when he said, "Remember the Sabbath and keep it holy."

Rabbi #1: So how does the Lord want us to keep it holy?

Rabbi Chhhh: I think he wants us to eat Swiss cheese.

Rabbi #3: Why do you say that?

Rabbi Chhhh: Because Swiss cheese has holes.

Rabbi #1: That's holey, you idiot.

Rabbi #4: The commandment says holy.

Rabbi Chhhh: Oh . . .

Rabbi #3: Jesus . . .

Rabbi Chhhh: Excuse me for breathing . . .

Rabbi #1: So how *does* the Lord want us to keep it holy?

Rabbi #4: Maybe we should spend the day praying . . .

Rabbi #1: And not working . . .

Rabbi Chhhh: And decorating our homes with glossy, spiny leaves that have whitish flowers and red berries!

Rabbi #3: Why, pray tell?

Rabbi #1: That's holly. We're talking about holy.

Rabbi Chhhh: Oh . . .

Rabbi #4: Jesus . . .

Rabbi #3: G-d help us all . . .

Rabbi #1: So how does the Lord want us to keep it holy?

Rabbi Chhhh: What if we spell holy chhhholy?

Rabbi #1: Get this moron out of here!

Rabbi #2: Hey, stop pushing . . . !

Rabbi #4: Grab his legs!

Rabbi Chhhh: I hate you guys!

TALMUDIC WISDOM

While there are literally hundreds of proverbial adages contained in the Talmud, its oral tradition and argumentative method of debate make it an ever-evolving tome. Therefore, what are now considered to be sagacious pearls originally went through what was essentially an editing process over the course of many centuries.

To illustrate this, here are a few examples of Talmudic sayings along with the original translations prior to refinement.

TALMUDIC SAYING	EARLIER VERSION
Rather to skin a carcass for pay than be idly dependent on charity.	Rather to skin a carcass for pay than to beat the hell out a blind man and make off with his wallet.
Hold no man responsible for what he says in grief.	Never hold a grieving man whose pants are down around his ankles.

Every blade of grass
has its Angel that
bends over it and says
"Grow. Grow."

He who gives
should never
remember, he who
receives should never
forget.

Living well is the best
revenge.

Hey, don't even think
about walking your
dog on our lawn!

He who receives
an STD should
remember who
he got it from and
give that name
to the health
department ASAP.

That's right, I live in
a bigger house than
you. Eat your heart
out, sucker!

THE FIRST MILLENNIUM

As millennia go, the first millennium C.E. was a hell of a millennium for the Jewish people. Three out of four Jews now lived outside Judea, which was now called Palestine. And for a people that had once been so mighty, it was also kind of a bummer than there were only four Jews left.

Just kidding! There were considerably more Jews than that, and most of them believed they were the Messiah. The Nazarenes were backing this one guy, maybe you've heard of him, but after the destruction of the Second Temple it seemed like maybe the world was ending and all kinds of turkeys came out of the woodwork, making all kinds of outrageous claims. The Roman emperor Hadrian generally responded to these claims by having these guys and all their followers killed. He also outlawed circumcision, maybe because he felt so bad about killing so many Jews that he figured he'd throw them a bone.

Without a homeland or a temple, the rabbis focused on studying the Torah and the oral traditions that had been handed down by Moses, passing from one generation to the next like an endless game of telephone, so that a once simple and commonsense teaching such as "don't eat a raw pig" eventually became so garbled and bizarre that it involved numerous sets of cutlery and took forty-nine days to repeat.

Finally, the rabbis realized that passing down the oral tradition was insanely time consuming—particularly the practice of starting over from the very beginning if you forgot anything. Many people dropped dead of old age before the rabbis even got to the juiciest parts of the oral tradition. And so around 200 C.E., Yehuda haNasi ("Judah whose name looks like a typo") had the bright idea of writing it down.

The result was the Mishnah ("That which is taught by repetition. By repetition. By repetition. That which is taught by repetition"). If Judaism, to this point, had been an all-in-one 1950s-style home phonograph cabinet, the Mishnah was a Walkman. It turned Judaism into a portable culture, and although hipster types never stopped moaning about the vastly superior warm, analog sound of the oral tradition, everybody else realized the tremendous advantage of the fact that unlike a rabbi, you could shut up a book.

You could also tuck it under your arm whenever you had to flee from persecution, and since Jewish life for the next eighteen hundred years was going to involve a lot of that, the Mishnah was right on time. Especially since, in the fourth century, Roman emperor Constantine converted to Christianity, bringing much of the empire with him. This was wholly unprecedented and astonishing—as if Derek Jeter one day woke up and decided to get a Red Sox logo tattooed across his chest, and then every Yankees fan went out and did the same. It was also bad news for the Jews, as the upstart Christian faith had chosen to answer the question "What makes you guys different from the Jews, if you worship a Jewish dude?" with "Well, you see, we hate them—and we can prove it!" Soon there were laws against interfaith marriage, building synagogues, and even attending the comedy shows of a young Mel Brooks.

Meanwhile, empires continued to rise, splinter, and fall. The Roman one broke in two, the two started to fight each other, and the Jews got the hell out of Dodge, heading for what would surely be easy times in Italy, Spain, and Germany. Then, around 600 C.E., a new religion called Islam began to emerge in the Middle East, and by the eighth century the Islamic empire was bigger than the Roman one had ever been and 90 percent of Jews were living under its rule.

Muslims considered Jews and Christians to be fellow "people of the book"—Islam considers the Torah and the Bible holy scriptures—and they dug the Jews for their scholarship and the ease with which they shrugged, learned Arabic, and adapted to life under yet another government. The Jews generally did better under Islamic rule than Christian, even though taxes made it hard for them to own land—pushing them away from farming and toward professions such as merchant, weaver, and orthodontist. They also couldn't ride horses—not that they wanted to—and their houses had to be smaller than their Muslim neighbors', which kept the heating bills down. Occasionally, there were forced conversions and property seizures. But despite all this, it was still definitely way shittier when Christians ran the show.

Eighth-century Spain was particularly good, for the Jews and for everybody else. In fact, it's known as the Golden Age of Spain, after Mort Golden, who ran a popular delicatessen. Jews from all over the Islamic world moved there, and Spain supplanted Persia as the global center of Jewish culture and study. Jews could own land and work in any field they wanted—though very few chose to work in an actual field—and there was a rich intellectual, scientific, and artistic life that transcended all sectarian boundaries.

This lasted until the Christians reconquered Spain in 1150, ushering in what is known as the Real Turd of an Age of Spain. Goodbye, landowning and professional freedom. Moneylending, humor writing, and perhaps pushing the odd cart full of rags or other such crap were the only jobs left. The great rabbinical school we forgot to mention in the previous paragraph closed, leaving only a few superstar rabbis like Rashi and Gershom with the juice to exert far-reaching influence in western Europe, which they exercised by issuing edicts on obscure Talmudic practices. This passed for entertainment at the time.

Oh, and then there were the Crusades! Pope Urban II, who was a real schmuck even for a pope, decided that it was time to reclaim Palestine by killing or converting the Muslims who controlled it. The Christians decided to start their raid closer to home, by slaughtering the Jews in their midst—maybe because getting to Palestine was such a schlep, or maybe because the Jews weren't allowed to own weapons and thus made for a low-impact warm-up massacre. This kind of thing kept happening, Crusade after Crusade. Often, the slaughter was fueled by blood libels about how matzoh was made from the blood of Christian babies, which was easier to believe than it would have been to confront the very real vampire crisis.

Luckily, though, there was always somewhere to run—some country that welcomed the Jews and their economy-stimulating brand of trading and moneylending moxie. Plus, if the Jews got too powerful or were owed too much money, you could always just seize their property, banish them, or kill them. It was a win-win. Some variation of this played out in England, France, Spain, Portugal, IHOP, Germany, and Italy. Sometimes, the Jews would be invited back to their land when whatever asshole king had banished them died.

In Spain, the first violence against Jews had flared up in 1391, but after weathering the usual attacks (or leaving for North Africa), a lot of Jews decided to go along to get along and converted to Christianity... or did they? Maybe they didn't! Maybe they were secretly still practicing their religion, so quietly and harmlessly that it was nearly impossible to tell! Luckily, in 1480 Queen Isabella found a solution to this vexatious nonproblem. It was called the Spanish Inquisition, which sounds like it should refer to some kind of innocuous question such as "What's in this gazpacho?" but actually involved investigating every single *converso* by means of a secret police force run by the Catholic Church, seizing the children of anybody found to still be Jewish and handing them over to be raised by monks and nuns, then torturing the adults until they confessed. The rest of Europe, looking on at these brutal new methods, decided they looked super fun and got in on the action.

In 1492, it all came to a head: Spain gave the Jews four months to convert to Christianity for real or leave with nothing but the clothes on their backs. To the Spaniards' surprise, the Jews left—two hundred thousand of them. Many went to Portugal, only to be kicked out a few years later. Others headed to the Netherlands, and still others went to Turkey, where they were welcomed by a sultan who was not an idiot and allowed them to establish "Sephardic" communities throughout the Ottoman Empire—in Greece, Iraq, Egypt, Palestine, and so on. Those communities flourished for hundreds of years. You know, like, until the early 1940s.

THE KABBALAH

Needless to say, no guide to Judaism would be complete without discussing Kabbalah—the ancient Jewish study of mysticism.

THE GOLEM

Of all the supernatural creatures in Jewish folklore, the golem is basically the only one. A golem is a giant humanoid creature created out of mud, usually by a rabbi. The Hebrew word for "truth" is written on its forehead, bringing it to life. When the golem has accomplished its task—which is often the defense of the Jewish people (as was the case with the Golem of Prague, widely considered to be the Michael Jordan of golems) but can also include manual labor (as was the case with the Golem of Chelm, generally thought of as the Scottie Pippen of golems) or merely going on bagel runs (which was the sole function of the Golem of West Palm Beach, known as the Michael Jordan When He Tried to Play Baseball of golems)—the aleph is erased from his forehead, changing the word "truth" to "death" and causing him to return to a state of vacant immobility, like a toddler in front of a television.

Over the centuries, the golem has taken on various metaphorical meanings. Sometimes a golem grows uncontrollable and/or kills its creators, which conveys the important lesson "do not make giant killer mud zombies." Other golems have been heroic defenders, boorish bozos (note the similarity of "golem" to "goyim"), and even tragic victims of unrequited love (meh). And you can't spell "Frankenstein's monster" or "artificial intelligence" without some of the letters in "golem." And without all of them, you cannot cheer on the director of *Young Frankenstein* should he happen to be running a marathon, as unlikely as that may be.

For complete instructions on how to construct an uncontrollable and psychotically violent golem of your own, please turn to Appendix H.

DISCUSSION QUESTIONS FOR "THE GOLEM"

- If you could command your own personal golem to kick the shit out of anybody, who would you pick?
- What about after Mel Gibson?

ISRAEL

For Jews, Israel is the Promised Land—the land that G-d gives to the Jewish people in the Book of Genesis, which states:

> *On that day the Lord made a covenant with Abram and said, "To your descendants I give this land, from the Wadi of Egypt to the great river, the Euphrates—the land of the Kenites, Kenizzites, Kadmonites, Hittites, Perizzites, Rephaites, Amorites, Canaanites, Girgashites and Jebusites."*

Don't get us wrong: it was very generous of G-d to give this land to the Jews. The only teensy little technicality was that—as Genesis notes—the land was already occupied by the Kenites, Kenizzites, Kadmonites, Hittites, and a half dozen other ites. Imagine being told that you had won a house in a lottery, but when you entered your new home, you found Amorites in the attic, Kadmonites in the kitchen, Perizzites in the parlor, and a Girgashite in the master bathroom depositing a big old Girgashit. That was the awkward situation that the Jews faced when they arrived in the Promised Land.

Which brings us (we are skipping some parts) to the year 1948. At that time what is now Israel was part of a territory called Palestine, which contained both Arabs and Jews but was governed by the British. There was a lot of tension in Palestine because the Jews and the Arabs hated each other, and everybody, including the camels, hated the British.

Finally, Britain decided enough with the tension already and got the United Nations to divide Palestine into two states, one for the

Arabs and one for the Jews. The problem was that instead of creating rational, militarily defensible borders for these states, the United Nations created the map by feeding two different colors of jelly beans to a cat and then inducing it to throw up on a piece of paper. This was the result:

As you can see, the two nations were all mixed up with each other. Parts of each nation were on strips of land so skinny that a person could accidentally violate a border merely by having an erection.

Nevertheless, the Jews decided to make a go of it, and on May 14, 1948, Israel declared its independence. This was followed by an era of peace and tranquility lasting for nearly forty-seven seconds, at which point Israel was attacked by troops from Egypt, Syria, Jordan, Iraq, Yemen, Morocco, Saudi Arabia, Mordor, and the Idaho National Guard.

That was the beginning of the 1948 Arab-Israel War, which was followed by the Six-Day War, the Yom Kippur War, the St. Patrick's Day War, the War When Moshe Lost His Pants, and the War Where Everybody Went to the Front via Uber. Israel won all these wars, because militarily the Israeli armed forces are the Harlem Globetrotters of the Middle East. Also, enemy tanks can never penetrate more than a few miles into Israel because the Israeli drivers refuse to yield to them.

As of this writing, Israel has not been involved in any major military conflicts for a period of several weeks, although there is still a lot of tension in the Middle East. For this reason, many people are reluctant to visit Israel. In fact, however, Israel is one of the safest nations on earth, according to statistics that we plan to search for later on Google. So you should definitely go. In the reassuring words of the Israeli minister of tourism: "What's the worst that can happen?"

You will find that Israel is a modern, bustling nation of nearly nine million people from a wide variety of ethnicities, religions, and political views, united by the common belief that you, personally, are in their way. So at first glance, Israelis may seem brusque, even rude. But appearances can be deceiving. Native Israelis call themselves "sabras," after the Hebrew name for cactus fruit: they may be prickly on the outside, but on the inside they are susceptible to aphid infestation. The main thing to remember is, every Israeli has a unique story to tell. Do not get them started.

FACTS ABOUT ISRAEL

Official Language: Hebrew
National Anthem: "Hatikvah" (Literally: "We Will Rock You")
Form of Government: Shouting
Climate: There is no way to tell. It's in Celsius.
Economy: They make a living.
Currency: The shekel
Seriously? Yes! The shekel!
Unit of Measurement: The Whole Megillah
Wi-Fi Password: MoshesPants

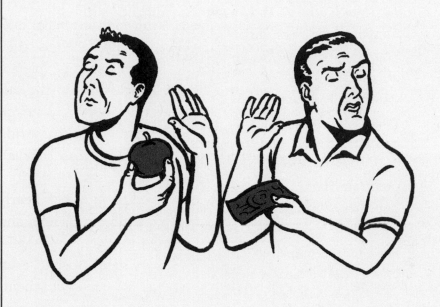

BARGAINING IN ISRAEL

Bargaining is an ancient tradition in Israel, dating back to the time of Moses, who was able to bargain G-d down to just the Ten Commandments. This was fortunate because G-d originally wanted thirty-five commandments, including "No robe, no service" and "Thou shalt not pee in the shower."

In modern Israel, it's an accepted practice to bargain for almost everything. If you pay the asking price for something without bargaining, you could be seen as a schmuck. But before you try your hand at bargaining, you need to be aware that there is a definitive protocol to follow. To understand how it works, let's consider a hypothetical scenario in which you're at a supermarket checkout counter:

YOU (PLACING A GRAPEFRUIT ON THE COUNTER): How much for this grapefruit?

CASHIER (LOOKING AT THE PRICE STICKER ON THE GRAPEFRUIT): Three shekels.

YOU: Three shekels? For a grapefruit? What am I, a schmuck?

CASHIER: That's the price.

YOU: I'll give you one shekel.

CASHIER: The price is three shekels.

YOU: Okay, two shekels. But that's as high as I will go.

CASHIER: The price is three shekels.

YOU: Okay, I'll think about it. *(You set the first grapefruit aside and place a second grapefruit on the counter.)* How much for this grapefruit?

CASHIER: Also three shekels.

YOU: Three shekels! For a grapefruit? What am I, a schm . . . *OW!*

The reason you say "OW" at this point in the scenario is that you have been shot in the leg by an Israeli soldier in line behind you, with the full support of all the other Israelis in your vicinity. So this scenario teaches us that the supermarket is not one of the places where you're supposed to bargain.

Where you *are* supposed to bargain is in Israel's many street markets. If you want to bargain "like a native," here are some tactical tips:

Do not appear to be too eager to buy.

Your opening offer should be half of the vendor's opening price.

Be courteous but firm.

Do not be afraid to express polite skepticism regarding claims made by the vendor, especially if he is selling alleged "antiquities."

Be prepared to walk away at any moment.

Let's see how you would employ these tips in a negotiation with a typical street-market vendor:

YOU: How much are you asking for these sandals, bearing in mind that I do not appear to be too eager to buy?

VENDOR: For these, seventeen hundred shekels.

YOU: That's too much. I will pay you ... hang on ...

VENDOR: In case you are wondering, half of seventeen hundred is 850.

YOU: In that case, my courteous but firm opening offer is 850 shekels.

VENDOR: But sir, these sandals belonged to Jesus!

YOU: Wait, *the* Jesus?

VENDOR: Yes! And he took excellent care of them! Note the condition! Very little wear!

YOU: Pardon my polite skepticism, but these sandals say "China" on the bottom.

VENDOR: Yes, because they were a gift to Jesus from the Three Wise Men, who were from China, as they clearly state in their song, "We three kings of Orient are."

YOU: Okay, but I am prepared to walk away at any moment.

VENDOR: You bargain like a native employing tactical tips! I have no choice but to accept your shrewd offer of 850 shekels.

YOU: It's a deal.

VENDOR: So for the two sandals at 850 shekels each, your total is ... let me see ... *(taps calculator)* seventeen hundred shekels.

YOU: Wait, what?

VENDOR: For the pair. Surely you do not want to split up the pair, sir! Not the sandals of Jesus!

YOU: I suppose not.

THE HISTORY OF BAGELS

The story of the bagel—that quintessential Jewish food—begins in the seventeenth century in a small village in Poland, where two brothers, Jacob and Mordecai, were struggling to make a living as bakers. In hopes of improving their business, they decided to come up with a new product. They tried baking bread into different shapes, including a triangle, a pentagon, and a trapezoid, but none of those caught on with their customers.

Then one day Jacob happened to glance out the window as a peddler was passing by, pushing a cart that had two big brown wheels. Suddenly Jacob had an idea.

"Mordecai, come here!" he shouted, for in this part of seventeenth-century Poland everybody spoke English.

"What is it, brother?" said Mordecai.

"Look!" said Jacob, pointing outside.

Mordecai looked, and gasped. "That's it!" he said.

"Yes!" said Jacob. "It's the shape we've been searching for!"

The two brothers hugged each other joyfully, then eagerly set about creating their new product, which was bread baked in the shape of a peddler.

They called it the "breddler."

Jacob and Mordecai stayed up all night and baked seventeen dozen breddlers. They sold a total of one, which was purchased, in an act of mercy, by their mother. She bit off the peddler's head, chewed it for several minutes, spat it out, and demanded a refund.

Utterly discouraged, Jacob and Mordecai quit the baking business and started an abacus-repair company that would eventually become International Business Machines. So for a time there was no village bakery. But then, as fate would have it, an enterprising young baker named Henrik arrived in the village with his new bride, Esther, a dairy farmer's daughter whose entire dowry had been paid to Henrik in the form of a 250-pound schmear of cream cheese. Henrik realized that this cheese was going to spoil unless he could come up with some kind of baked good that it could be spread on. And so he invented the bagel.

Henrik's invention was an immediate hit, except with the village asshole, who insisted that the only place you could get a decent bagel was New York City.* But everybody else loved Henrik's invention. "This is WAY better than the breddler" was a common reaction.

Pretty soon the bagel had spread throughout Poland, and then to the rest of Europe, except England, which was not as receptive because nobody there had teeth. In 1802 the bagel was introduced to the New World by the legendary Jewish sea captain Solomon "Long Tallit" Weisenberg, whose merchant ship, *The Steep Discount*, crossed the Atlantic carrying eighteen tons of bagels—in the form

---

* This was also the village asshole's stance regarding pizza and Chinese restaurants.

of six three-ton bagels—which served as both ballast and a source of many hearty breakfasts for the crew.

The bagel soon spread throughout the American colonies, thanks largely to the efforts of a man known as Johnny Poppyseed, who spent years walking from settlement to settlement handing out bagels to grateful pioneers, who used them as horseshoes. But the growing influence of the bagel in North America did not come without mounting tension, finally resulting in the French and Indian War (1754–63) which broke out when French bakers started putting cinnamon and raisins in the bagels they were trading with the Indians. As you can imagine, this really pissed off the Indians. In the words of Iroquois chief Running Nose, "If I wanted a damn cinnamon bun, I would have asked for a damn cinnamon bun."

So in essence the war was a struggle between good (bagels without cinnamon and raisins) and evil (bagels containing cinnamon and raisins). Unfortunately for humanity in general, evil prevailed, and the door was opened for unscrupulous bakers to defile the once-pure bagel recipe with all kinds of unnatural ingredients—a defilement that continues to this very day in the form of alleged "bagels" containing blueberries, chocolate chips, sprinkles, kale, and numerous other pollutants. Also, there are people who think nothing of putting jelly on a bagel. You read that correctly: *jelly on a bagel*. It's not a scone, people! Nor is it a doughnut! It's a *bagel*, and there should be standards.

Peanut butter is a different matter. Peanut butter is mentioned approvingly by name fourteen separate times in the Old Testament.

BAGELS IN THE CIVIL WAR

Bagels played a crucial role in the Civil War, used by both sides as food as well as munitions. The turning point in the war came when the South, because of northern ship blockades, ran desperately low on lox, thus forcing Confederate troops to top their bagels with grits, which was disgusting, although everyone agreed it was still better than jelly.

Fact: Abraham Lincoln wrote the Gettysburg Address on a bagel, but he absentmindedly ate half of it before delivering his speech, which is why it ends in midsentence.

BAGELS IN MODERN TIMES

In modern times bagels can be found all over the world. Bagels have even gone into space! That's right: In 2008, an American astronaut carried eighteen bagels up to the International Space Station. Some scientists had reservations about this, as their calculations showed that if one of the bagels were to somehow get loose, it could plummet to Earth with enough kinetic energy to destroy Cleveland. But then they decided they could live with that.

MODERN JEWISH HISTORY

In the 1500s many Jews settled in Poland, and over the next several centuries they spread throughout Europe, usually living in isolated communities called shtetls (Hebrew for "little shtet"). These Jews enjoyed a mostly peaceful existence punctuated by periods of getting killed by their neighbors. To pass the time between mass slaughters they developed their own language, Yiddish, which is a mixture of Hebrew, German, Polish, Russian, Esperanto, Sarcasm, and Despair. Many colorful Yiddish words have come into common use in American English, the most popular being:

- *Schmuck*—A klutz. (Usage example: "What a schmuck!")
- *Chutzpah*—A large loogie. (Usage example: "Someone has ejected a chutzpah onto my cardigan!")

- *Klutz*—A schmuck. (Usage example: "What a klutz!")
- *Oy vey*—Golly. (Usage example: "Oy vey, I could sure go for some hominy grits!")
- *Kvell*—Sound made by a swooping eagle as it grasps a salmon in its talons. (Usage example: "KVELL!") Also a kind of doughnut.
- *Putz*—A klutz or schmuck. (Usage example: "What a putz that klutz is, the schmuck!")

In the eighteenth and nineteenth centuries, different groups of European Jews pursued very different paths concerning their relationship with their Gentile neighbors. On one end of the spectrum were the Orthodox Jews, who rejected assimilation and continued to strictly observe traditional Jewish religious rituals and customs such as wearing big black hats, growing long beards,* and just generally acting—we say this without passing judgment—weird. On the other end were European Jews who rejected many aspects of Judaism and sought to "fit in" with the dominant Christian culture by consuming Jell-O, playing golf, taking mambo lessons, and using the expression "swell." These efforts to assimilate resulted in these Jews being totally accepted, even beloved, throughout all of Europe.

Ha ha! Such kidders we are! In fact, no matter how hard the Jews tried to not seem too Jewish, many Gentiles continued to regard them as outsiders and blamed them for basically everything bad that happened, including humidity.

As the twentieth century dawned, anti-Semitism was on the rise throughout Europe, and the situation of Jews became increasingly precarious. Some Jews emigrated to Palestine, where they eventually founded the state of Israel. (See "Israel.") (Or don't see "Israel." We're not your mother.) But many Jews remained in Europe, hoping that the situation would improve.

Spoiler alert: the situation did not improve.

---

* Even the women.

LAST THURSDAY

A priest, a minister, and a rabbi walked into a bar. The bartender said to the priest, "What will it be?" "I'll have a beer," said the priest, and the bartender gave him a beer. The bartender then asked the minister, "And what would you like?" The minister said, "I'll also have a beer," and the bartender gave him a beer. Then the bartender looked at the rabbi and asked, "Why did you kill Christ?" and smacked him across the face with a pitcher of sangria. So anti-Semitism is still a bit of a problem.

OY

"Oy" is an interjection borrowed from Yiddish that's used to convey dismay, pain, or exasperation.

It's a common misconception that "oy" is a shortened version of the exclamation "Oy vey." However, just as "Don't" is a contraction of "Do not," "oy" is, in fact, a contraction for the Eastern European shtetl lament "Oh no, my wife's mother is coming to live with us, my store just burned down, and it really burns when I pee, why, G-d, why!"

FEH

A Yiddish word used as an expression of annoyance or disgust.
Its origin dates back to Rabbi Mordecai Feh (389–323 B.C.E.),
who was renowned throughout his Eastern European shtetl
for being annoying and disgusting.

The Talmud documents Rabbi Feh's history with lyrics to
the once popular children's Jewish ghetto playground song...

"Who's the rabbi with crumbs in his beard!"

"Feh!"

"Who's the rabbi whose breath is weird?"

"Feh!"

"What rabbi is annoying?"

"Feh!"

"What rabbi is disgusting?"

"Feh!"

"Who's the rabbi whose cat is plaid?"

"Feh, Feh, Feh, Feh, Feh!"

FREQUENTLY ASKED QUESTIONS ABOUT THE WORD "TUMULT"

Q. People actually ask questions about the word "tumult"?

A. Tons.

Q. Exactly who are these people?

A. Ones who say it sounds like a Yiddish word. Like "hectic," "svelte," "concoction," "bench," "lentil," and "Jewish."

Q. Wait a second! "Jewish" isn't a Yiddish word?

A. Nope. It's an English word.

Q. For what?

A. Yiddish.

Q. So "Yiddish" is a Yiddish word?

A. Not really.

Q. But you just said . . .

A. It's actually a German word.

Q. For what?

A. Yiddish.

Q. So what's the Yiddish word for "Yiddish"?

A. There is none.

Q. Why?

A. Well, since the Germans had already come up with a word, the Jews turned their attention to other matters, such as deciding to put a "C" in front of "Hanukah" but not in front of "Henry Kissinger," who was much more Jewish than Charlie Sheen, who's a raging anti-Semite who doesn't deserve that "C."

Q. I don't know about this . . .

A. What don't you know?

Q. That story sounds a little far-fetched.

A. "Far-fetched" is another English word that sounds Yiddish. And since you're the Q part of this Q&A, could you please keep what you have to say in question form?

Q. Like on *Jeopardy*, that game show starring Alex Trebek?

A. "Trebek" also sounds Yiddish, does it not?

Q. I'm sick of this inane conversation.

A. In question form, please.

Q. What if I told you that you're an idiot and I refuse to talk to you any longer?

A. Excellent.

THE HOLOCAUST

We will not mince words: the Holocaust was bad for the Jews. And yet, despite the horrific carnage, despite the vile and grotesquely evil dogma enthusiastically embraced by so-called civilized nations, despite the inconceivable misery and the unbearable pain inflicted upon millions—a pain that can still be felt today; a pain that can never truly be erased from the Jewish consciousness—there was still, in the end, a positive side of the Holocaust.

THE POSITIVE SIDE OF THE HOLOCAUST

Now that we're thinking about it, the Holocaust didn't really have a positive side. Forget we even brought it up.

JEWS IN EUROPE TODAY

There are an estimated seventeen Jews living in Europe today. They would prefer that we not reveal where.

QUIZZES, QUESTIONS & ANSWERS, LISTS, AND OTHER ATTEMPTS TO MEET OUR CONTRACTUALLY OBLIGATED WORD COUNT

ARE YOU AN ANTI-SEMITE?

Find out by answering these eight questions.

1. Do the Jews control Hollywood?
If you answered YES, you are an anti-Semite. Conspiracy theories about the Jews secretly wielding power over various industries have long been used to paint the Jewish people as menacing, puppet-string-holding outsiders intent on molding culture to our insidious needs.

If you answered NO, you are an anti-Semite. All the major Hollywood studios—Universal, MGM, 20th Century Fox, etc.—were founded by Jewish immigrants from eastern Europe, virtually inventing the film business. And that's without even getting into our outsized presence as writers, actors, producers, and directors. Failing to recognize the enormity of our contribution is frankly disgusting.

2. Do you believe that Jews are opinionated, pushy, and prone to butting in?
If you answered YES, you are an anti-Semite. This stereotype of the aggressive Jew, always talking, arguing, and sticking his giant schnozz in everyone else's business, is deeply offensive.

If you answered NO, you are an anti-Semite, and you ought to think long and hard about your stereotypical belief that the Jews are clannish, secretive, and reclusive, as these are all untrue and hurtful.

3. A Jewish fellow, Schwartz, buys a house right next door to Rockefeller—a nearly identical house. What's more, he hires the same gardener and buys the same car. One day

Rockefeller sees Schwartz coming out of his house, and he says, "Hey, Schwartz, you think you're as good as me, don't you?" "No," says Schwartz, "I think I'm better than you." Rockefeller, furious, demands to know why. "Well," says Schwartz, "for one thing, I don't live next door to a Jew." Is this funny?

If you answered YES, you are an anti-Semite. There is nothing funny about the struggles of Jewish people with assimilation and internalized self-hatred, and this so-called joke is a tragic illustration of just how corrosive such feelings can become.

If you answered NO, you are an anti-Semite. Only someone with a bias against the Jewish people could fail to see the humor in the way Schwartz turns Rockefeller's anti-Semitism against him. Perhaps someday someone will do the same to you.

4. All things being equal, would you be more inclined to have your criminal defense handled by a Jewish lawyer?
If you answered YES, you are an anti-Semite. While flattering, the stereotype that Jews make the best lawyers ultimately does us a disservice by ignoring the myriad reasons we were locked out of other professions and reinforcing the notion that all Jews are bookish and argumentative.

If you answered NO, you are an anti-Semite. The Jewish aptitude for law—and our significant contribution to it—is grounded in a long, rich history stretching all the way back to the days of Moses, and failing to acknowledge this is deeply problematic.

5. Who would you say is "more Jewish": the legendary twelfth-century rabbi Moses Maimonides, the famous singer Sammy Davis Jr., or the esteemed author Saul Bellow?
If you answered this question at all, you are an anti-Semite.

6. Is your favorite bagel flavor (a) poppyseed, (b) blueberry, (c) onion, (d) salt, or (e) cinnamon raisin?

If you answered b or e, you are an anti-Semite. If you answered a, c, or d, you may well be an anti-Semite but we'll have to find another way to prove it.

7. Do you feel that you couldn't possibly be anti-Semitic because you are, in fact, Jewish?
The fact that you are taking this quiz despite being Jewish means that you are anti-Semitic.

8. Has Judaism always struck you as ancient, mysterious, and beautiful—a world rich with ritual and history, a religion that has managed to sustain itself in the face of unbelievable oppression and seemingly insurmountable odds?
If you answered YES, you are an anti-Semite. We encourage you to examine your fetishistic obsession and your patronizing attitude, and recognize how shockingly sick they are.

If you answered NO, you are an anti-Semite. Your disdain for Jewish culture and history is egregious and boycott-worthy.

COMMON QUESTIONS ABOUT JUDAISM

Hi.
Hi.

Did you have a question?
Sorry, what?

I happen to be one of the world's foremost authorities on Judaism and I'm here today answering questions, as part of my plea bargain. So did you have a question?
Oh! Sure! I have tons. For starters, why don't Jews believe in Jesus?

Jews love Jesus. He's one of our own, and so were his parents and his disciples and basically everybody he ever met right up until the end there. We're happy for his success, just like we're happy for Seth Rogen's. We just don't believe that either one of them is the Messiah, because we believe that when the Messiah shows up, he'll usher in a new age of peace and love. Has that happened yet?
No, I guess not. Heck, I just got in a knife fight with some jerk in the parking lot on my way in here.

Right. Exactly. Did Jesus break it up?
No.

Didn't think so.
So what's Jewish humor?

Here's a better question: What's Christian humor? Have you ever even heard that phrase?
Never.

Jewish humor is characterized by a number of character-istics, as well as some traits. To learn more, you can turn to Appendix C of this book, which is just Mel Brooks's home phone number.
So what's this "Chosen People" stuff all about?

I'll grant you that it's an unfortunate turn of phrase. In fact, it almost seems designed to make enemies. But it basically just means *chosen to follow the Torah*, not cho-sen in the sense of *the rest of you losers didn't get picked*. Also, chosen isn't just chosen: the question is, *chosen for what*? And the answer, some Jews think, is *to be a light unto the world*.
And how's that going?

Eh.
Am I allowed to use the phrase "Jewed him down" to illustrate my prowess in negotiating a lower price?

Nah, you could get smacked for that.
Are you allowed to use it?

Oh, yeah, I use it all the time.
I bet your mother hates that.

Yeah, she does.
Why are there so many Jewish lawyers?

You ever read the Talmud?
I think it's pretty obvious that I have not.

The Talmud is basically one endless argument over the most infinitesimal and nuanced aspects of a sprawling, totalized system of law. It's the third most important book in Judaism, after the Torah and this one. That ought to tell you something. Also, for a good portion of our history, we've been unable to own land and forced to live in urban centers, so we learned to do jobs you could do there—law, medicine, stand-up comedy.
Oh, so does that also explain why Jews aren't usually thought of as big outdoorsmen?

No. We lost our appetite for camping much earlier—after wandering in the desert outside Egypt for forty years and then getting kicked out of every major country in Europe. Not Sweden.

I said major country.
Can you convert to Judaism?

Sure! And once you convert, you're no more or less Jewish than anybody else.
Presumably you're more Jewish than, like, Mitt Romney.

You know what I mean. To convert, you'll need to find a rabbi to study with. Some rabbis may turn you away three times before they accept you, to test your resolution. Other rabbis may accept you, then make you perform manual labor for several months before teaching you anything, but then when they do start teaching you, you realize that all the manual labor actually was teaching you something all along, like Mr. Miyagi in *The Karate Kid*. When your rabbi decides you're ready for conversion, you'll appear before a *beth din*, a religious court made up of three rabbis, who will attempt to ascertain your level of sincerity and study. How?

If it's an Orthodox conversion, they might have you read a passage from the Torah, offer commentary on Rashi's interpretation of it, make you play "Dayenu" on the shofar, demand to know who begat Zilpah, challenge you to down a steam tray of gefilte fish in seven minutes or less, and ask you to make several snide remarks about the goyim. If it's a Reform conversion, they will simply ask if you know that Scarlett Johansson is Jewish. Once you have passed your conversion test, you will be taken to the mikveh for a ritual submersion and, if you're a man, circumcised.

What if I'm already circumcised?

You can still expect to be ritually poked in the junk until you bleed. Finally, you'll learn the secret Jewish handshake and be given a special code.

Whoa, what does that do?

It gets you onto the Wi-Fi.

Is it true that Jews have horns?

Some do, yes. Notable Jews with horns include Mezz Mezzrow, Herb Alpert, Herbie Mann, Stan Getz, Paul Desmond, Benny Goodman, John Zorn, and Joshua Redman.

What about Kenny G?

What about him?

Is it true that Jews use the blood of Christian babies to make their matzohs?

This is known as "blood libel," and it's definitely one of the top two gluten-related falsehoods used to persecute Jews—the other being "desecration of the host," which (really) is the claim that Jews like to break into Catholic churches and stick pins into the communion wafers in

order to torment Jesus. Both are absurd, of course. Have you ever tasted matzoh? Do you think it would taste like low-quality particleboard if it contained something as rich and flavorful as human blood?

Does an international cabal of globalist Jews control the media, banking, and world government?

No, but we do have the delicatessen industry on lock. Anything else?

I think I'm done. Will you validate my parking?

You did a great job parking.

TEN PEOPLE WE WISH WERE OR WERE NOT JEWISH, AND TEN PEOPLE YOU DIDN'T KNOW WERE OR WERE NOT JEWISH, AND TEN PEOPLE WE ARE THRILLED AREN'T JEWISH

Although the Jews are known as the Chosen People, we wish Hashem had also chosen the following:

1. LeBron James
2. Billie Jean King
3. Michelle Obama
4. The Geico Lizard
5. Bruce Willis
6. Mongo Santamaria
7. David Bowie
8. Chow Yun-fat
9. Dave Barry (sober)
10. Lassie

On the other hand, the Yiddish expression "Shondah for the goyim" refers to something or someone that brings shame upon the Jews, and thus joy to non-Jews. Here is a list of people we could've lived without being members of the Tribe, because they are . . . wait for it . . . *bad for the Jews:*

1. Roseanne Barr
2. Drake

3. Meyer Lansky
4. Harvey Weinstein
5. Pee-wee Herman
6. Lena Dunham
7. Bernard Madoff
8. David Berkowitz (Son of Sam)
9. Stephen Miller (Son of G-d knows who)
10. Tie: Gwyneth Paltrow/the shark from *Jaws*

Then there are the people you thought were Jewish, but aren't:

1. Bob Hope
2. Tina Fey
3. Julia Louis-Dreyfus
4. David Letterman
5. "Weird Al" Yankovic
6. Lily Tomlin
7. Anybody funny who isn't black, basically
8. The Illuminati
9. Tie: Warren Buffett/Elijah Wood
10. That lady Esther from Accounts Receivable

And the people you didn't know were Jewish, but are:

1. Paula Abdul
2. Marilyn Monroe
3. Philip Roth
4. Daniel Radcliffe
5. Amar'e Stoudemire
6. That lady Carla from Accounts Payable
7. Pope Innocent XI
8. José Bautista
9. tie: Barry Manilow/Chewbacca
10. Harry Houdini

And then there are the people who, were they Jewish, would be a huge embarrassment:

1. Tim Tebow
2. Andrew Jackson
3. The 1989 Detroit Pistons
4. Hurricane Sandy
5. Vanilla Ice
6. Dave Barry (drunk)
7. The California Raisins
8. The Kardashians
9. Rudy Giuliani
10. James Woods

A CONVERSATION WITH
THE AUTHORS

Moderated by Rabbi Schmooley Weiskopf

Rabbi Schmooley Weiskopf: Welcome to the annual Conference of American Jewish People. I'm Rabbi Schmooley Weiskopf, and the three men onstage with me need no introduction, particularly since their bios are in the program, so instead let me use this time to talk about the wonderful party tents of the local party tent company that sponsored this panel. Are you in need of a tent in the greater Phoenix area? For a wedding, a Bar Mitzvah, maybe a fund-raiser? Look no further than Hauppman's Party Tents. They've got you covered! Ha ha. Get it? Who said a rabbi can't do shtick? But in all seriousness, as Mr. Hauppman was just telling me backstage, he and his family have always cared tremendously about Jewish education and the Jewish community, and seen it as their responsibility, as successful local businesspeople, to give back as much as they can. So you should rent his tents! If you mention this event, Hauppman's Party Tents is offering a 5 percent discount on all tents, and that also applies to silverware rental. So how about a round of applause for Mr. Hauppman and Hauppman's Party Tents? Okay! Thank you very much. Their website is www-dot-hauppmanspartytents-dot-pizza. Apparently, someone already has www-dot-hauppmanspartytents-dot-com and dot-org. Okay! So! Today we have three very funny guys with us, and here they are!

Adam Mansbach: Is there . . . a question?

Rabbi Schmooley Weiskopf: No! Just talk!

Alan Zweibel: Often, a moderator will prepare some questions.

Dave Barry: Okay, I guess I'll go first. I think I need to explain why I'm part of this, because I'm not Jewish. In fact, both my father and his father were Presbyterian ministers. But, being honest here, there's not a lot of Presbyterian humor. I actually don't know if there are any jokes featuring Presbyterians. What would they say? They'd be like: "So this Presbyterian walked into a bar, but he immediately realized his mistake and left."

My point is, I'd have no material, writing about my own heritage, so when Adam and Alan begged me to help them write a book about Judaism, I said yes. I actually know a little about the Jewish faith. My wife, Michelle Kaufman, is Jewish. She's actually Cuban-Jewish, or, as they call themselves, "Jewban." My joke about them is: "They didn't come here on rafts; they parted the Caribbean."

See? It's much easier with Jews.

I haven't converted to Judaism, but Michelle and I belong to a temple in Coral Gables; our daughter, Sophie, is Jewish, and had a Bat Mitzvah, which could very well still be going on. Also, my son, Rob, married a Jewish woman, Laura, and they asked me to be the sandek, or baby-holder, for the bris of my grandson Dylan. That was probably the most courageous thing I have ever done.

Also, I have attended many High Holiday services, some of which lasted longer than the Korean conflict. So as I see it, even though I am not, technically, Jewish, I am involved enough in Judaism to qualify as a member of the International Zionist Cabal that secretly controls the entire world. Any day now I expect somebody to teach me the secret handshake.

Adam Mansbach: That thing I did just now, right before we got onstage? That *was* the secret handshake.

Dave Barry: So *that's* why you asked me to bring—and here I'm quoting your text to me—"the blood of a Gentile infant."

Adam Mansbach: That was actually for something else. But anyway, my way into this book was a little different from Dave's. I have four Jewish grandparents—none of whom, to my knowledge, ever set foot in a synagogue, and at least two of whom were actively hostile toward organized religion.

My parents, out of guilt, sent me to a Jewish Sunday school that was unaffiliated with any temple—it was like the So You Think You Might Be Jewish Sunday School and Grill, and it was run out of an off-brand community college. Hebrew class was optional. I actually got kicked out of this school for—this is true—singing the Bon Jovi song "Livin' on a Prayer" into the microphone at an all-school assembly instead of the phonetically spelled-out Hebrew prayer I was supposed to read. They called my house and were like, "Maybe Adam ought to think about trying one of the other religions; they all have their good points." I got kicked out of a summer camp that same year. It was kind of a rough year.

Anyway, many years later I was doing research for a novel that wasn't really intended to be about anything Jewish, but it was about people based on my grandparents. And I came to understand that regardless of whether they were religious, being Jewish defined, in large part, who they were. Their opportunities, but also their sensibilities. And the same is true of me. I feel connected to the part of Judaism that gives us "two Jews, three opinions," the part that sets up arcane, unbreakable, pain-in-the-ass rules and then immediately turns its attention to finding loopholes and workarounds for every one of those rules.

As far as this book, I do a lot of work with the elderly—reading in nursing homes and so on. And coincidentally, I was volunteering in the old-age home where both Dave's and Alan's children live. They're getting up there in age, but they were kind enough to introduce me to their fathers, and from there we started to collaborate.

I grew up watching Alan's work on *Saturday Night Live* and reading Dave's columns, so to actually work with them, as you can imagine, has been incredibly disappointing. I really wish I'd met them when they were still funny.

Dave Barry: If being younger than I am means singing "Livin' on a Prayer" at a school assembly, then I don't ever want to be younger than I am.

Rabbi Schmooley Weiskopf: What about you, Alan? Would you sing "Livin' on a Prayer" at a school assembly?

Alan Zweibel: I have. Twice. Once wearing what Madonna wore in that classic video. The second time wearing what Jesus's mom wore in that classic manger. By the way, Rabbi Schmooley Weiskopf, how come it took you this long to include me in this conversation? I've been sitting here getting weepy wondering why you let Dave and Adam blather on as they did. Do you not care for me?

Rabbi Schmooley Weiskopf: You appear to be confusing "Livin' on a Prayer" by Bon Jovi with "Like a Prayer" by Madonna. For the record, neither of these acts is Jewish.

Alan Zweibel: Oh . . .

Dave Barry: Alan is an idiot. I say this as a friend.

Adam Mansbach: He is also easily startled by loud noises.

Alan Zweibel: So is this the reason why I wasn't included in this conversation earlier? Flimsy excuse. As if none of you ever mistook Jesus's mom for Jon Bon Jovi.

Dave Barry: I rest my case.

Rabbi Schmooley Weiskopf: For the record, Jesus's mother was Jewish. Moving along, what was the most unexpected thing you learned in researching these books?

Alan Zweibel: Jesus's mom was Jewish?

Adam Mansbach: That's a great question, Rabbi. A surprising amount of research goes into the crafting of every single cheap dick joke we write. Personally, I was surprised to learn about the Nephilim, a race of giant immortal beings who mate with human females in the Book of Genesis, creating a race of long-lived mortals, and then pop up again as occupants of Canaan when Moses sends his spics to check the place out. There's a lot of disagreement about what the hell that's all about, and if they were angels or giants or if it's all just a weird mistranslation. But mostly, I find it fascinating that the Torah is chock full of incredibly weird shit like this that nobody really talks about, and meanwhile there's a giant, incredibly boring body of rabbinical literature about which grains you're allowed to eat during Passover.

Dave Barry: And even when people *do* talk about the weirdness, they don't *really* talk about it. Exhibit A is when G-d tells Abraham to sacrifice his son, Isaac, and Abraham is like, "Okay, G-d! I'm on it!" Even Isaac seems kind of blasé about it, saying nothing when HIS FATHER IS TYING HIM UP AND GETTING OUT A KNIFE. This story, in my view, tends to be glossed over. Sometimes the rabbi will say something about G-d testing Abraham's faith, but WHAT KIND OF INSANELY CRUEL TEST IS THAT? TO TELL A FATHER TO SLIT HIS SON'S THROAT AND HE ALMOST ACTUALLY *DOES* IT? AM I USING TOO MANY CAPITAL LETTERS HERE?

Adam Mansbach: I assume you are addressing that last question to the person who will eventually be transcribing these oral remarks for publication?

Dave Barry: I forgot we were being oral. Sorry!

Adam Mansbach: Alan insisted on it, as he is functionally illiterate. Also, without wishing to be indelicate, have you noticed anything remarkable about his head?

Dave Barry: I really don't think we should discuss that. Alan is very sensitive about the size of his head, which is enormous, like a UPS truck with ears. The less said about it the better, is my feeling. And by "it," I mean "Alan's gigantic head."

Adam Mansbach: I'm sorry I even brought it up, Dave. At least, I think it's Dave. As Alan is sitting between us, I can only go by the sound of your voice.

Alan Zweibel: My head is not *that* big. You just assume that because of the moss growing on its north side. But we all have that, right? Right?

Rabbi Schmooley Weiskopf: Maybe it's the wine talking, but I would like to ask each of you to talk about Jewish humor. What is it, and why has it had such an outsized influence?

Dave Barry: I think at least part of it is that humor is an important psychological mechanism for coping with misfortune, and Jews have had a LOT of misfortune, especially when you compare them to the Presbyterians. The same is true of the Irish, who've had more than their share of rough times and are also funny. Of course, the British can also be funny, and they controlled most of the world for several centuries. So to sum up this response: Beats me.

Adam Mansbach: I think there is a certain sensibility to a lot of Jewish humor. It's biting but also self-deprecating. It often relies on a certain kind of wordplay, a certain kind of misdirection. It uses the tropes of anti-Semitism to defang the anti-Semite. It tends to be understated, but make understatement its own kind of flourish, if that makes sense. I also may have just described all humor. Or maybe those elements have suffused all other humor.

Alan Zweibel: Here's a Jewish joke: A young man who's never had sex before gets married and on his wedding night sneaks a call to his mother and asks her how to make love. And his mother says, "It's easy. All you have to do is take the longest part of your body and put it into where your wife goes to the bathroom." So ten minutes later he calls his mother and says, "Okay, my leg is in the toilet, now what do I do?"

Adam Mansbach: That is the worst joke I've ever heard.

Rabbi Schmooley Weiskopf: I'm confused why you say that's a Jewish joke.

Alan Zweibel: Oh, because the man who installed that toilet was Jewish . . . Why are you guys shaking your heads and whispering things about me?

Dave Barry: That joke—and I do not say this lightly—is so bad it could be Presbyterian. Is there any more wine?

Adam Mansbach: I want to state for the record that Alan was forced on us by the publisher.

Rabbi Schmooley Weiskopf: Perhaps we should take some questions from the audience. Yes. In the back.

Audience Member: My daughter is so funny. I mean, she is really, really talented. And I just wanted to know—

Adam Mansbach: Flattered, but spoken for.

Audience Member: What?

Adam Mansbach: Oh, no, I thought . . . Sorry. Please, go on.

Audience Member: So, I want to know from you three: Do you think she should be a screenwriter? Or maybe a stand-up comic? Or a humor writer?

Alan Zweibel: Well, first of all, it's so refreshing to meet a Jewish woman who thinks her daughter is talented.

Audience Member: Yeah, I mean, she is so talented. And *funny*. I think she'd make a great screenwriter.

Dave Barry: How old is your daughter?

Audience Member: She's forty-nine.

Dave Barry: And has she ever written a screenplay?

Audience Member: No.

Dave Barry: Then my guess is that she doesn't want to be a screenwriter.

Rabbi Schmooley Weiskopf: Any other questions? Yes, in front.

Audience Member: I knew Mel Brooks's mother. And once she invited me over for dinner. And she said to me, "What do you think of my boy Melvin?" And I said, "He seems like a wonderful son." And then we had dinner. And it was lovely.

Dave Barry: The ending needs work.

Alan Zweibel: You must be a real hit at parties with that story.

Rabbi Schmooley Weiskopf: Any other questions?

Audience Member: Is it true that if a person bites you it's more dangerous than if a dog bit you?

Dave Barry, Adam Mansbach, Alan Zweibel: Schmooley . . .

Rabbi Schmooley Weiskopf: Okay, one last question.

Audience Member: When Superman gets a boner . . .

Dave Barry, Adam Mansbach, Alan Zweibel: Jesus, Schmooley!

Rabbi Schmooley Weiskopf: Fine, no more audience questions . . .

Dave Barry: So we talked about Jewish humor, and we know there are a lot of Jews in the comedy business. But what about music? Look at all the successful Jewish composers—Leonard Bernstein, Stephen Sondheim, Irving Berlin, Marvin Hamlisch, Jerome Kern, George Gershwin, Ira Gershwin, Elvis Gershwin . . . the list goes on and on. Why is that? Please don't tell me it has to do with chanting the Torah. With all due respect, that is not musical.

Alan Zweibel: I beg to differ—the Torah is very musical if you beat a drum with it.

Adam Mansbach: It has nothing to do with chanting the Torah and everything to do with the fact that the Jews have been an urban people for the last however many centuries—sometimes because we weren't allowed to buy land, sometimes because the professions we were allowed to practice were citified ones, sometimes because there was no train service from Ellis Island to Connecticut.

What does this have to do with music? Music, especially in this country, is the most successful example of the whole "melting pot" concept. And the city is where the melting happens. Also the pot. By "the city," of course, I mean New York City, not, like, fucking Dallas. So you've got Jews living in high-density areas, poor areas, smashed up against neighbors of all creeds and races, everybody with their own musical traditions, and they start to bleed into each other and you get mash-ups and cross-pollinations.

Because you are old and square, Dave, you mentioned a bunch of dead or nearly dead composers. But you could have just as easily rattled off a list of Jewish musicians and producers who made significant contributions to Latin music in America from the 1950s on—guys who could read charts and play parts and thus got gigs in Tito Puente's band or Mongo Santamaria's . . . and to bring it full circle, those bands ended up playing the resorts in the Catskills all summer, because Jews were on the cutting edge of all the Latin dance crazes, from the mambo to the cha-cha to whatever.

Or you could have mentioned hip-hop, which I realize you have never heard of, but a very high percentage of credible white people in hip-hop are Jews. I realize this answer was not that funny, so let me also add that Alan once showed up to a public talk we were doing with his sweater on backward, and when I alerted him to this fact, he suggested that the audience could just stand on the other side of him.

Rabbi Schmooley Weiskopf: Alan, since you clearly have very little to add here, might I inquire as to whether you've been comfortable at the hotel we booked you?

Alan Zweibel: Hardly . . .

Rabbi Schmooley Weiskopf: You're kidding. What seems to be the problem?

Alan Zweibel: That's why I haven't been saying much. I was up half the night bailing water from my bathroom.

Rabbi Schmooley Weiskopf: The toilet overflowed?

Alan Zweibel: My sink. The faucet came off in my hand when I made the unheard-of move of trying to turn off the water after I brushed my teeth. And when I finally did fall asleep I was awakened about a half hour later by two bugs the size of my high school.

Rabbi Schmooley Weiskopf: Oh, my . . .

Alan Zweibel: By then the sun was coming up, so I ordered room service, and about an hour later, after watching the TV that for some ungodly reason only showed *Golden Girls* in Spanish, my breakfast of cold coffee and gray eggs arrived.

Rabbi Schmooley Weiskopf: This is the first complaint I've ever heard about that hotel.

Alan Zweibel: Hard to believe.

Rabbi Schmooley Weiskopf: We put all our authors at that hotel. Elie Wiesel loved that hotel.

Alan Zweibel: My guess is that hotel is the second-worst place he ever slept in.

Dave Barry: Thank you, Alan, for that insight into the relationship between Jews and music. I want to say, in defense of my own cultural background, that we Presbyterians have also played a significant role in the development of hip-hop, as we can see by the results of this Google search:

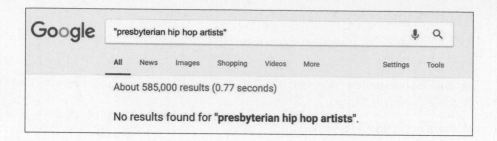

Alan Zweibel: Very impressive . . .

Adam Mansbach: Dave, your command of this medium is truly astounding. To my knowledge this is the first time anyone has successfully incorporated a sight gag such as a Google search into a live onstage conversation, which I would like to remind you yet again is what we are currently engaged in.

Alan Zweibel: I agree with Adam. I just tried to Google "Famous Haitian Astronauts" and was surprised to learn that there aren't any.

Adam Mansbach: That is hardly my point, Alan. But fine. If this discussion is degenerating into cheap sight gags, here is a photo of my daughter wearing an adorable *Go the Fuck to Sleep* onesie.

Rabbi Schmooley Weiskopf: How adorable. I bet they make a lovely baby shower gift, perhaps paired with your classic book of the same name.

Alan Zweibel: Nobody likes a kiss-ass, Weiskopf.

Rabbi Schmooley Weiskopf: That's not what your mother said.

Dave Barry: Speaking of Jewish mothers, how about we speak of Jewish mothers? Are the stereotypes true? I don't personally have a Jewish mother, but I do have a Jewish mother-in-law, and all I can say is that she is a fine person who may very well read this book.

Alan Zweibel: I have a Jewish mother who . . . how should I word this . . . who still has her end of my umbilical cord attached to her.

Rabbi Schmooley Weiskopf: Interesting metaphor, Alan.

Alan Zweibel: It's not a metaphor, Schmools. That's why my mother blames me for her never owning a proper-fitting bathing suit.

Rabbi Schmooley Weiskopf: Please don't call me Schmools.

Dave Barry: So here's a question from the Presbyterian community that I think you guys are uniquely qualified to answer: Is it true that Jewish men have small penises?

Adam Mansbach: It may interest you to know that Nazi propaganda—this is true—often referenced the exceptionally large penises of Jewish men. This also seems like a good time to tell that joke about how circumcision caught on because a Jewish woman won't touch anything that's less than 20 percent off.

Alan Zweibel: Hey, you know why circumcision caught on?

Adam Mansbach: I just told the joke, Alan. That was me telling the joke.

Dave Barry: Adam, just so I understand: You're citing, as your authority, *Nazi propaganda?*

Adam Mansbach: I was trying to keep this civilized. But I can take my pants off, if you prefer.

Dave Barry: Sure!

Rabbi Schmooley Weiskopf: I'm afraid I can't allow that.

Adam Mansbach: Every time I try to take my pants off, some rabbi gets in the way. It's been like this my whole life.

Alan Zweibel: That reminds me of a joke.

[Forty-five seconds of silence]

Rabbi Schmooley Weiskopf: Perhaps you'd like to tell it?

Alan Zweibel: What a lovely idea! An elderly gentleman walks into a confession booth, and he says to the priest, "I met a woman yesterday. She's twenty-two. Beautiful. I asked her out to dinner—she said yes! And then I took her home, and we made love all night! And again in the morning!"

The priest says, "And you'd like to absolve yourself of this sin, my son?"

"Absolve myself? Ha! I'm going back home to get it on with her again. Heck, I'm not even Catholic."

"So why are you telling me this?"

"I'm telling everybody!"

Adam Mansbach: Oh, so we're doing this now? Okay. So it's famine times in Poland, and these two Jews hear a rumor that the Catholic Church will give you money if you convert. They draw straws, and the loser, Moshe, goes into the church while his friend waits outside in the snow. After almost an hour, Moshe comes back out. "What happened?" his friend asks eagerly.

"You know, it wasn't that bad." Moshe shrugs. "They gave me some wine, and some crackers, and they made me say some prayers."

"But did you get the money?" his friend asks impatiently.

Moshe shakes his head slowly. "Is that all you people care about?"

Dave Barry: A Jewish guy is shipwrecked for twenty years on a desert island. Finally, he's rescued. The sailors who find him are amazed at what he's made of the island, and they ask him for a tour. "Sure," he says. "Here's the synagogue. And here's a little store I built, so I can sell myself coconuts and pineapples and stuff, and here's my house, and here's another synagogue . . ."

The sailors are like, "Hold on, why are there two synagogues?"

"That one I pray in, and THAT ONE I WOULDN'T BE CAUGHT DEAD IN!"

Alan Zweibel: Two Gentile businessmen run into each other on the street.

The first one says, "How's business?"

And the second one says, "Great!"

Adam Mansbach: This guy, Reuben, is walking down the street in Brooklyn, when suddenly he's approached by a stranger.

"Hey, mister," the stranger says, "you wanna buy an elephant? I got a genuine African elephant, five hundred dollars, this is a once-in-a-lifetime deal, you're never gonna get a chance like this again."

"No, thanks. Me and my whole family, we live in a two-bedroom tenement. I don't have room for an elephant."

"Yeah, but mister, this is a one-of-a-kind elephant, and oy, what a bargain. If you don't buy this elephant you're gonna regret it the rest of your life."

"Buddy, I can't afford an elephant, I got nowhere to put an elephant. My kids are scared of dogs, never mind elephants, and my ceilings are only seven feet high. Thanks, but no thanks."

He walks away, and after a moment the stranger calls after him: "Two elephants for seven-fifty!"

Reuben spins back around: "*Now* you're talking!"

Dave Barry: A young priest in Vatican City notices a blind beggar sitting just outside his church holding a cup with a Star of David scrawled on it. "Excuse me," he says. "My friend, I don't know if you realize, but you're in Vatican City, the capital of the Catholic world. And you're holding a cup with a Jewish star on it. And to make matters worse, not ten feet away from you is another beggar with a cross on his cup. Not only will people not give money to you, they're going to give *more* money to him, just to spite you!"

The beggar with the Jewish star sits up and calls over to the beggar with the cross.

"Hey, Morty, look who's telling the Goldstein brothers about marketing."

Alan Zweibel: An elderly rabbi decides that before he dies, he has to find out what pork tastes like. So he drives a couple of hours away, sits down in the best restaurant in that town, and orders a whole suckling pig. No sooner does it arrive than he hears a horrified cry: "Rabbi Goldblatt! What are you doing?"

Goldblatt turns and sees one of his congregants.

"Silverman! Thank goodness you're here! Oy vey, this restaurant—I order a baked apple, and they bring me this!"

Adam Mansbach: There's a tailor named Rosenberg. One day, on his way to work, he hears the voice of G-d. And G-d says, "Rosenberg! Sell your business! Take it in cash!" Rosenberg is very startled, but this is G-d, so he sells his business that very day. He goes home, he eats dinner, he awaits further instructions. And sure enough, the voice of G-d returns. "Rosenberg! Go to Las Vegas!" Rosenberg books the next flight to Las Vegas. He steps off the plane, onto the tarmac, and the voice of G-d returns. "Rosenberg! Go to the black-jack table! Bet everything!" Rosenberg repairs to the nearest casino and plunks down his life savings on the blackjack table.

The dealer hands him his cards. Rosenberg has eighteen. The dealer flips his own cards—seventeen. Rosenberg is ecstatic—he's just doubled his life savings. But then the voice of G-d returns. "Rosenberg! Take another card!"

Rosenberg summons all his courage and taps the table. "Hit me." The dealer gives him a card. Bam! An ace! Nineteen! He breathes a huge sigh of relief. But then the voice of G-d returns. "Rosenberg! Take another card!"

People in the casino are beginning to stare at him. Rosenberg is sweating profusely. But he thinks of his ancestors, his traditions, and says, "Hit me!"

Bam! Another ace! Twenty!

The voice of G-d returns. "Rosenberg! Take *another* card!"

Rosenberg can barely bring himself to do it, but he taps the table. "Hit me."

Bam! Another ace! Twenty-one!

The voice of G-d returns.

"UN-FUCKING-BELIEVABLE!"

Rabbi Schmooley Weiskopf: You do an excellent voice of G-d.

Adam Mansbach: Thanks. It's kind of a specialty of mine.

Dave Barry: You do realize that we've now been sitting on this stage for seventeen hours?

Alan Zweibel: I have to pee. And not for the first time.

Rabbi Schmooley Weiskopf: But . . . you haven't left the stage.

Alan Zweibel: I'm a professional.

Dave Barry: Ew.

Adam Mansbach: Most of the audience appears to have left. Or died in their seats.

Alan Zweibel: What I think we're trying to say, Rabbi, is that perhaps it's time to bring this conversation to a close.

Rabbi Schmooley Weiskopf: Thank you all for coming! You've been a wonderful audience! Don't forget to buy the book!

Dave Barry: There's literally no one here.

Rabbi Schmooley Weiskopf: Buy two!

Adam Mansbach: I told you we shouldn't have hired a booking agent out of the phone book.

Alan Zweibel: Particularly the 1981 Paramus, New Jersey, phone book.

Dave Barry (*handing copper cups to Zweibel and Mansbach*): Here, have a Moscow Mule.

Adam Mansbach: Where did you get these?

Dave Barry: My suitcase is full of them. And all the bars are closed now, as it is three A.M.

(The authors stand.)

Woman in the Front Row: Wait! I'm still here, and I have some more stories about Mel Brooks's mother.

Dave Barry: Alan would love to hear them.

(Alan sits back down.)

Alan Zweibel: I'd love to hear them. Can you make it quick, though?

(Dave Barry walks offstage.)

Alan Zweibel: Adam, you're staying, right?

Adam Mansbach: Sure, sure. Wait here, I'll be right back.

(Adam Mansbach walks offstage.)

Woman in the Front Row: So. It's 1953. Or maybe '54. And my hairdresser, Sadie, she says to me . . .

(Rabbi Schmooley Weiskopf walks offstage.)

Alan Zweibel: I guess dying here beats going back to that hotel.

ACKNOWLEDGMENTS

Writing a book—like winning a Super Bowl, popping a back zit, or getting Cher stage-ready—is a team effort. Nobody does it alone.

This book is no exception: it would not have been possible without the help of many people, and the authors sincerely wish to thank them without in any way suggesting that they are legally entitled to compensation.

First and foremost, as happily married men who were fortunate enough to have found our "soul mates," we want to thank the women who have made such a difference in our lives: the Dallas Cowboys Cheerleaders. We could not have done it without you. Especially Tiffani.

We owe a huge debt of gratitude to the wonderful, always-helpful staff members of the Library of Congress. Any errors of fact in this book are totally their fault.

We also would like to thank our agents, but they have specifically requested that their names not appear in this book, so fuck them.

We thank the American Association of Rabbis, the Association of American Rabbis, the Associated American Rabbis of America, the Rabbinical Association of Rabbis of America, and the Pittsburgh Penguins. You are all amazing!

We thank the late Stephen Hawking. He knows why.

F. Scott Fitzgerald, Ernest Hemingway, Herman Melville, and William Faulkner are the names of just some of the authors that we can only hope to someday become more familiar with the work of.

We thank Julius Erving and the rest of the NBA-champion 1982–83 Philadelphia 76ers, especially Bobby Jones, who we believe never got the credit he deserved for his play coming off the bench.

A much-belated thank-you (and congratulations!) to Dr. Jonas Salk.

To Carly Simon for not spelling "You're So Vain" "You're So Vein" because that would have confused us to the point of delaying delivery of this book to our publisher.

We are grateful to the George Washington Bridge for not being parallel to the Hudson River because that would have been pointless.

Is Joey Buttafuoco still alive? If so, he has our sincere thanks.

Thanks also to the inventor of the umbrella for making the open side face down so we don't walk around collecting water.

We thank the Wright brothers, but not both of them. Just Orville. Wilbur knows why.

We thank Queen Elizabeth II for the delicious sandwiches.

Another person we would like to mention here is Johnny Weissmuller.

The efforts of the Mormon Tabernacle Choir have been invaluable in the completion of this work.

Our personal guru, Dr. Raam-Halumi Birdsong Bidet-Ginsberg, has overseen our spiritual development for more than twenty years. All blessings flow through him, the most exalted and munificent one.

A writer could not hope for sounder legal advice than that provided by Michael D. Cohen. He is more than a lawyer—he is a confidant and a dear friend.

The Schiller family, Michael, Antonella, and Leo, are more than just neighbors. They have brought us so many delicious meals that we have lost count, and this is especially impressive considering that we, the authors, live in three different states.

Had the three of us not been attending a Slayer concert at the Worcester Coliseum in 1989, we never would have met. Much love to our favorite band and city!

This book was made possible in part by a grant, but frankly we cannot remember who gave it to us or what we spent the money on.

Thank you to HBO for providing us with early access to the

final season of *Game of Thrones,* as well as to the secret season after the final season that will never be released commercially.

Our research assistant, Rabbi Menachem Sinowitz, deserves special praise for abandoning his post at Jerusalem's largest synagogue and his family to embark on this journey with us.

We feel that Gimli was an overrated member of the Fellowship of the Ring.

Our complete Fellowship of the Ring rankings are as follows: Frodo, Sam, Aragorn, Legolas, Pippin, Merry, Boromir, Gimli.

If you think about it, Gimli is the only member of the fellowship without a single signature achievement, unless you count pushing to travel through the Mines of Moria, and we all know how that turned out.

Oh, shit, we forgot Gandalf in the rankings. He's #1, obviously.

Our eternal gratitude to the Nyack Writers Conference, the Nyack Fire Department, the Nyack Game and Wildlife Department, the staff of the New Beginnings Wellness Clinic in Nyack, Judge Maria Gethelsmane of the Nyack Third Criminal Circuit, and especially John Kalamata of the *Nyack Weekly Gazette,* a man of class and discretion, for his decision not to further inflame the events of that week.

We thank whatshisname. The guy. With the hat. Right? Or was that the other guy? Whichever one it was, we thank him. But he needs to return the machete.

They say that comedy is tragedy plus time. We would like to thank them for saying that. We don't agree, but somebody has to say these things, and them has stepped up in a big way.

Astute readers will notice that large portions of this book have been lifted verbatim from the 1982 film *Conan the Barbarian* and the 1989 2 Live Crew album *As Nasty As They Wanna Be.* We are grateful to the copyright holders of these works for being asleep at the wheel.

Our helper monkey, Pogo, was an invaluable source of inspiration, mixed drinks, and thrown feces, and we would like to thank the St. Louis Zoological Institute for loaning him to us and also spearheading the efforts to find him when he disappeared, taking Alan's passport and a good deal of our petty cash with him. To assist with the search, please visit www.whereispogo.net.

Sometimes the difference between a bestselling book and a tax write-off for the publisher is as simple as a first-rate Lou Rawls impersonator. Thanks to We're Entertainment LLC of Trinidad & Tobago for making that happen.

A team is only as good as its weakest link, and we are truly blessed to have as wonderful, funny, and handsome a weak link as Alan Zweibel.

Thanks to the San Bernardino Institute for Primate Learning for providing us with a replacement helper monkey after the departure of Pogo. Irene was witty and conscientious—a true joy to work with right up until the day she, too, decided to strike out on her own in Adam's Audi A6 sedan, license plate CA 34DG22. Please visit www.whereispogo.net/irene to help bring her home.

Sometimes it takes a child to write a chapter nobody else feels like writing. Thanks to Viv Mansbach for tackling pages 34–47, 78–79, and 109–208 of this book.

Just when we thought no other organization would let us have a helper monkey, the Liberian Wildlife Jobs Training Initiative came up big. This book would be far different without the tremendous contributions of Raoul, and while we would certainly like to recover Dave's deep-sea fishing boat, we also feel that in a way, Raoul has earned his vacation. Please visit www.whereispogo.net/raoul to help.

While most scientists hold that the massive prehistoric shark known as megalodon (Carcharodon megalodon) went extinct in the late Pliocene era, we are among the minority who believe this giant killing machine merely adapted to lower and lower strata of the ocean and is still roaming the ink-black depths, feasting on smaller sharks, whales, and giant squid. Strangely, we find this notion comforting.

We salute the men and women of the Woodbridge Township, New Jersey, Fire Rescue team for the skill, courage, and—above all—patience they displayed in freeing Alan from the Wendy's restroom stall despite his inability to grasp the concept of "counterclockwise."

We'd like to thank this distinguished group of American industrialists, for continuing to work with Cuba, for the greatest period of prosperity in her entire history. Mr. William Proxmiro, representing the General Fruit Company; Messrs. Corngold and Dant, of the United Telephone and Telegraph Company; Mr. Petty, regional vice president of the Pan American Mining Corporation; and, of course, our friend Mr. Robert Allen, of South American Sugar. Mr. Nash of the American State Department. And Mr. Hyman Roth of Miami and Michael Corleone of Nevada representing our associates in tourism and leisure activities.

To the four chambers of our hearts for doing such a great job pumping blood 24-7.

To club soda for the great job it does removing stains when it's dabbed as opposed to being rubbed on the affected area.

To Abraham Lincoln's beard for covering what we understand to have been some very unsightly pockmarks.

To the island of Bora Bora for not calling itself Bora Bora Bora, because the authors firmly feel that two Boras are more than enough.

To anyone we may have forgotten: We didn't forget you. You have deliberately been snubbed.

Except for Yo-Yo Ma. That was an accident.

ABOUT THE AUTHORS

Dave Barry is a Pulitzer Prize–winning humor writer whose columns and essays have appeared in hundreds of newspapers over the past thirty-five years. He has also written a number of *New York Times* bestselling humor books, most recently Lessons from *Lucy: The Simple Joys of an Old, Happy Dog*. He is not personally Jewish but many of his friends are.

An original *Saturday Night Live* writer, **Alan Zweibel** has won numerous Emmy and Writers Guild of America Awards for his work in television, which also includes *It's Garry Shandling's Show* (which he cocreated), *Late Show with David Letterman*, and *Curb Your Enthusiasm*. He collaborated with Billy Crystal on the Tony Award–winning play *700 Sundays*, and he won the Thurber Prize for his novel *The Other Shulman*. Unlike Dave Barry, he has no Jewish friends.

Adam Mansbach is the #1 *New York Times* bestselling author of *Go the F*** to Sleep* and *You Have to F****** Eat*, as well as the California Book Award–winning novel *The End of the Jews*, a dozen other books, and the movie *Barry*. His work, which has been translated into more than forty languages, has appeared in *The New Yorker, The New York Times Book Review, Esquire,* and *The Believer* and on National Public Radio's *All Things Considered* and *This American Life*. Dave Barry and Alan Zweibel are his only friends.

ABOUT THE TYPE

This book was set in Duotype Allegro Grande Caramel, a typeface originally designed by Carl Hochenstein (1233–1301) for Pope Boniface VIII. Originally conceived as a private type for the pontiff's correspondence with his many illicit children, it was hand-cut for composition by Matisyahu Mandelblatt, the famous Lithuanian punch-cutter and mohel. Though modeled on the Aldine type used for Pietro Cardinal Anguila's treatise on cooking with lard in 1198, Duotype Allegro Grande Caramel is a thoroughly unique reworking of that venerable face. It is far more subtle than the Duotype Allegro Venti Skim, which gained popularity in the latter half of the sixteenth century but is frankly a bullshit font for fuckfaces. The Allegro Grande Caramel is distinctive for the sloping, highly erotic curves of its *S, P,* and *B,* and the full extension of its *Y,* which stretches an eighth of a centimeter past any other typeface of the era and caused five days of rioting when it was first introduced, resulting in the loss of seventeen lives and the burning of the west wing of the papal palace. The typeface is also notable for its complete lack of an *X,* interpreted by printing scholars as Mandelblatt's response to Boniface VIII's insistence on a 10 percent papal discount. More than six hundred other typefaces applied for inclusion in this book, and the selection process involved a traditional conclave in which the three authors, the publisher, the copy editor, a kosher butcher, two rabbis, a priest, and the only living descendant of Carl Hochenstein locked themselves in a paintball facility outside Reno, Nevada, to do battle on behalf of their preferred typefaces. Alan Zweibel accidentally shot himself in the face more or less immediately and had to be airlifted to a veterinary hospital for emergency cosmetic surgery, but thankfully this did not disrupt the conclave. In 1999, Duotype Allegro Grande Caramel was selected as one of *Smithsonian* magazine's prestigious Hundred Typefaces of the Millennium, and in 2007 it was given a star on the Hollywood Walk of Fame. In 2013, it was named Distinguished Typeface in Residence at Vassar College, and in 2021 it will be featured in the opening credits of *Jumanji 2,* starring Karen Gillan, Dwayne "The Rock" Johnson, and Jack Black.